BROTHER
A STORY OF AUTISM

Written by **BRIDGET HUDGENS**
and **CARLTON HUDGENS**

Art by **NAM KIM**

Colors by **FAHRIZA KAMAPUTRA**

Lettering by **TYLER SMITH**
for Comicraft

Zuiker Press

Los Angeles

BROTHER: A STORY OF AUTISM

Bridget and Carolton Hudgens
Photographs © 2019 Hudgens family

Written by Anthony E. Zuiker
Art by Nam Kim
Cover art by Garry Leach
Colors by Fahriza Kamaputra
Lettering by Tyler Smith for Comicraft
Designed by Roberta Melzl
Edited by Dave Elliott

Founders: Michelle & Anthony E. Zuiker
Publisher: David Wilk

Published by Zuiker Press
16255 Ventura Blvd.
Suite #900
Encino, CA 91436
United States of America

Visit us online at www.zuikerpress.com

ISBN 978-1-947378-08-7 (hardcover)

PRINTED IN CANADA
November 2019
10 9 8 7 6 5 4 3 2 1

DEDICATED TO ... every young person who needs to be reminded they are not alone.

HOPE lies within these pages.

ZUIKER PRESS

... is a husband and wife publishing company that champions the voices of young authors. We are an **ISSUE-BASED** literary house. All of our authors have elected to tell their personal stories and be ambassadors of their cause. Their goal, as is ours, is that young people will learn from their pain and heroics and find **HOPE**, **CHANGE**, and **HAPPINESS** in their own lives.

TEACHER'S CORNER

SHANNON LIVELY

Shannon Lively is a National Board Certified educator with a bachelor's degree in elementary education from the University of Nevada, Las Vegas, a master's degree from Southern Utah University, as well as advanced degrees in differentiated instruction and technology. In 2013, she was awarded the Barrick Gold One Classroom at a Time grant, and then chosen as Teacher of the Year. She is currently teaching fifth grade at John C. Vanderburg Elementary School in Henderson, Nevada.

WHY WE HONOR TEACHERS

We understand the amount of hard work, time, and preparation it takes to be a teacher! At Zuiker Press, we have done the preparation for you. With each book we publish, we have created printable resources for you and your students. Our differentiated reading guides, vocabulary activities, writing prompts, extension activities, and assessments are all available in one convenient location. Visit Zuikerpress.com, click on the For Educators tab, and access the **DOWNLOADABLE GUIDES** for teachers. These PDFs include everything you need to print and go! Each lesson is designed to cover Common Core standards and is aligned with the middle school curriculum. We hope these resources help teachers utilize each story to the fullest extent!

5

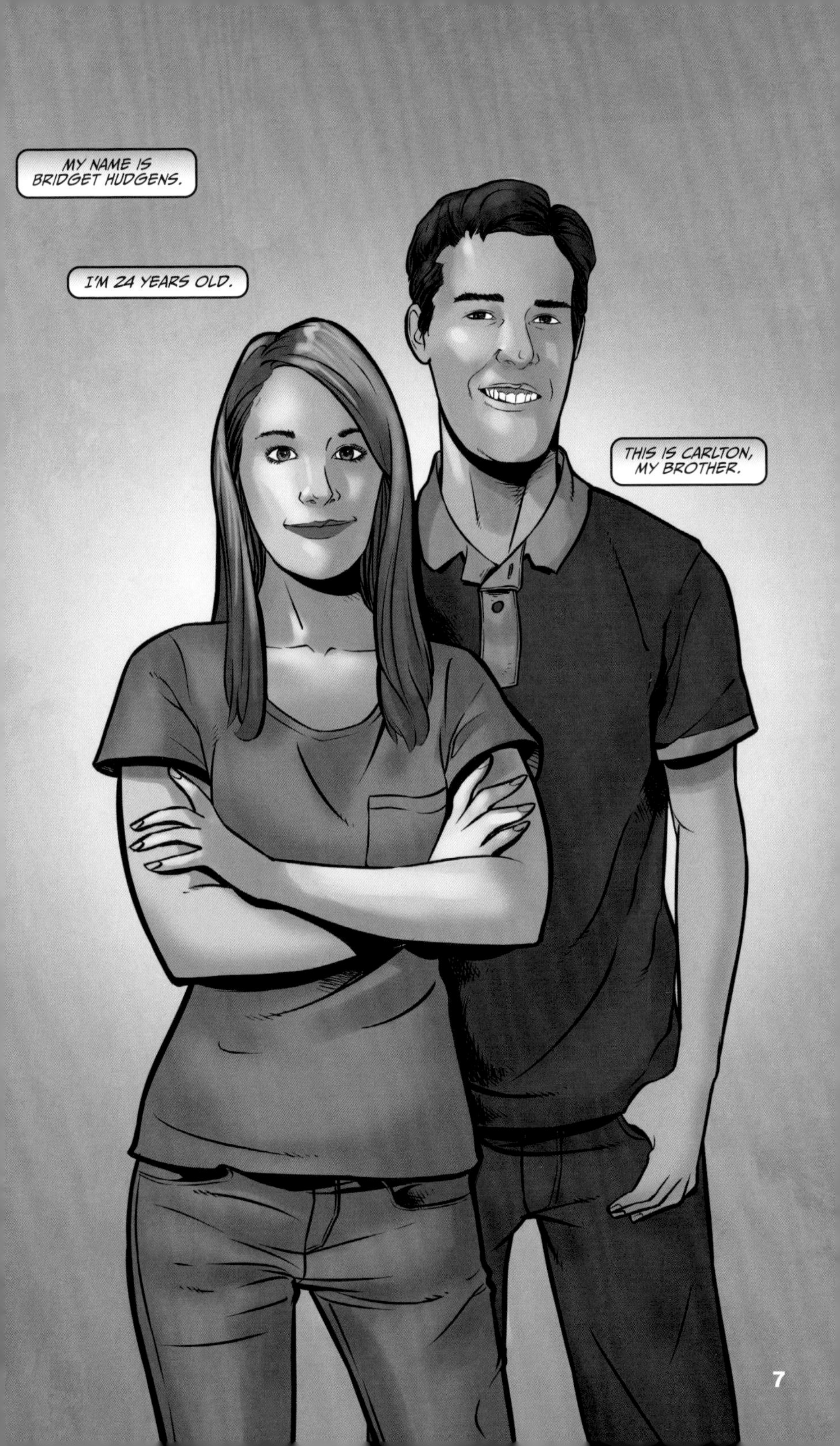
MY NAME IS BRIDGET HUDGENS.
I'M 24 YEARS OLD.
THIS IS CARLTON, MY BROTHER.

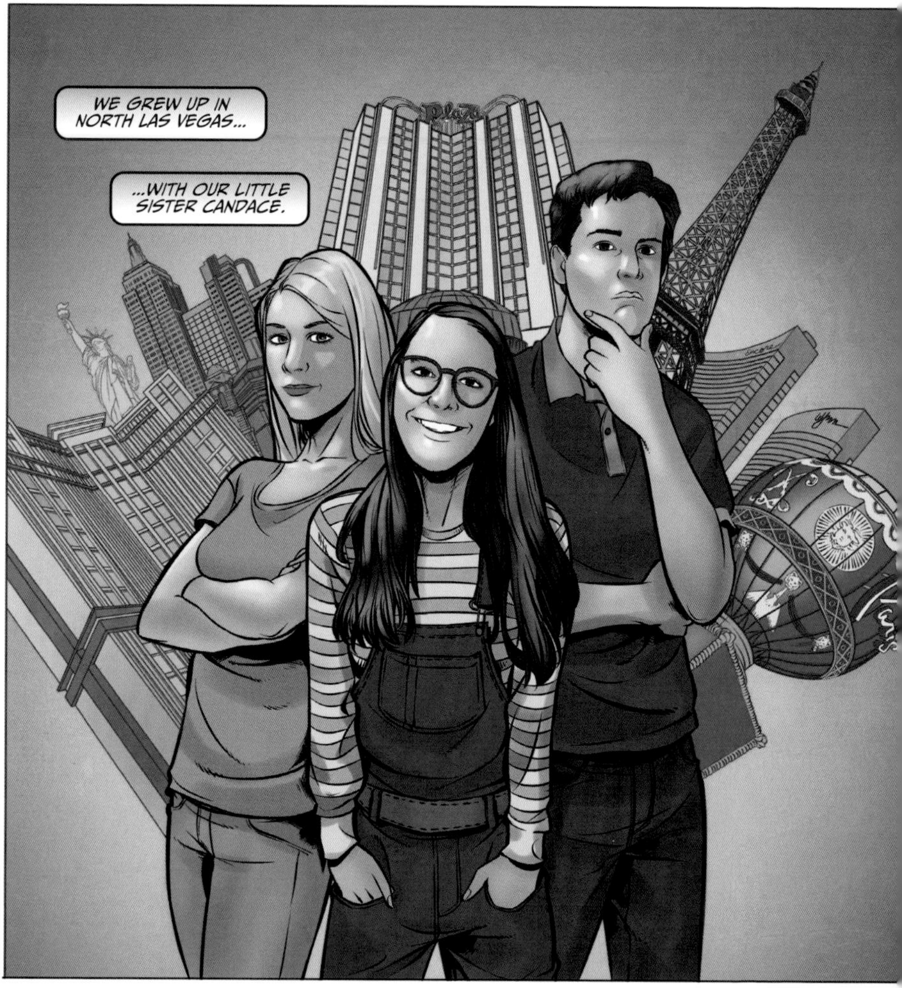
WE GREW UP IN NORTH LAS VEGAS...
...WITH OUR LITTLE SISTER CANDACE.

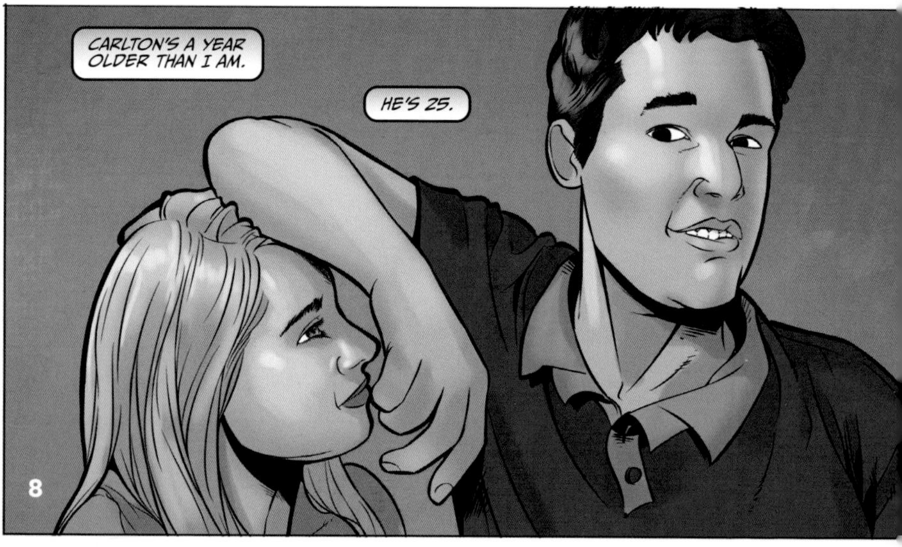
CARLTON'S A YEAR OLDER THAN I AM.
HE'S 25.

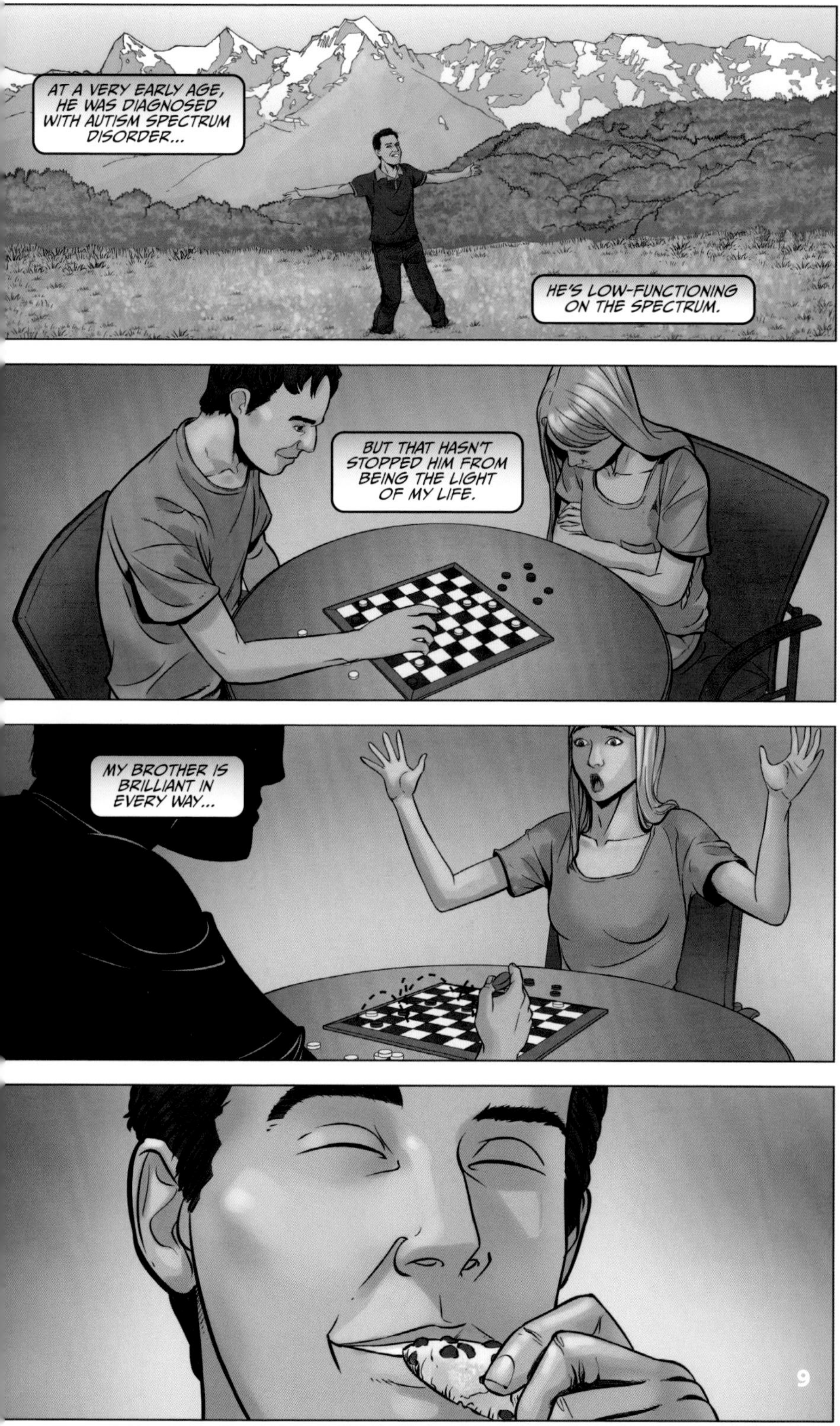
AT A VERY EARLY AGE, HE WAS DIAGNOSED WITH AUTISM SPECTRUM DISORDER...
HE'S LOW-FUNCTIONING ON THE SPECTRUM.
BUT THAT HASN'T STOPPED HIM FROM BEING THE LIGHT OF MY LIFE.
MY BROTHER IS BRILLIANT IN EVERY WAY...

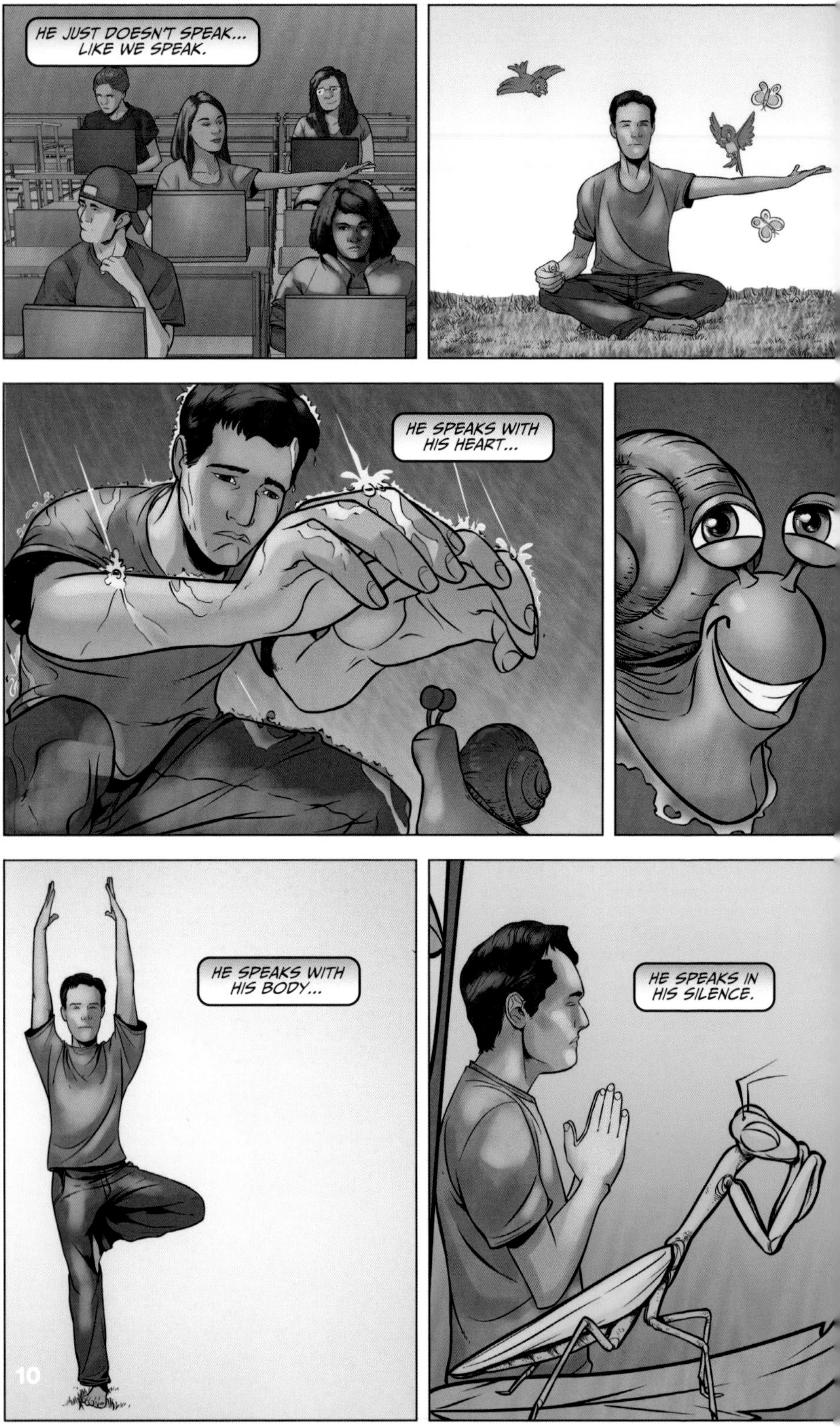
HE JUST DOESN'T SPEAK...
LIKE WE SPEAK.
HE SPEAKS WITH
HIS HEART...
HE SPEAKS WITH
HIS BODY...
HE SPEAKS IN
HIS SILENCE.

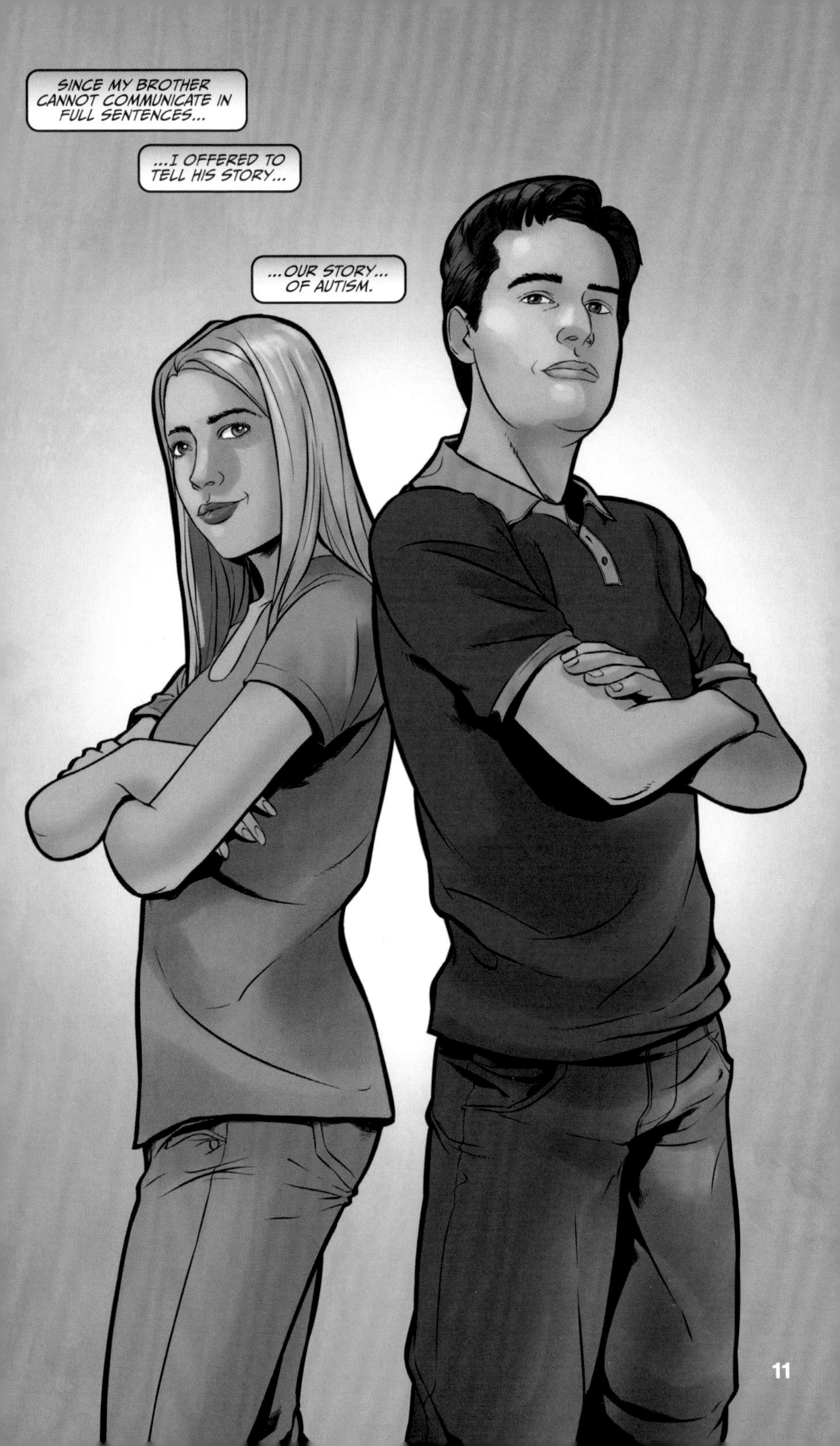
SINCE MY BROTHER CANNOT COMMUNICATE IN FULL SENTENCES...
...I OFFERED TO TELL HIS STORY...
...OUR STORY... OF AUTISM.

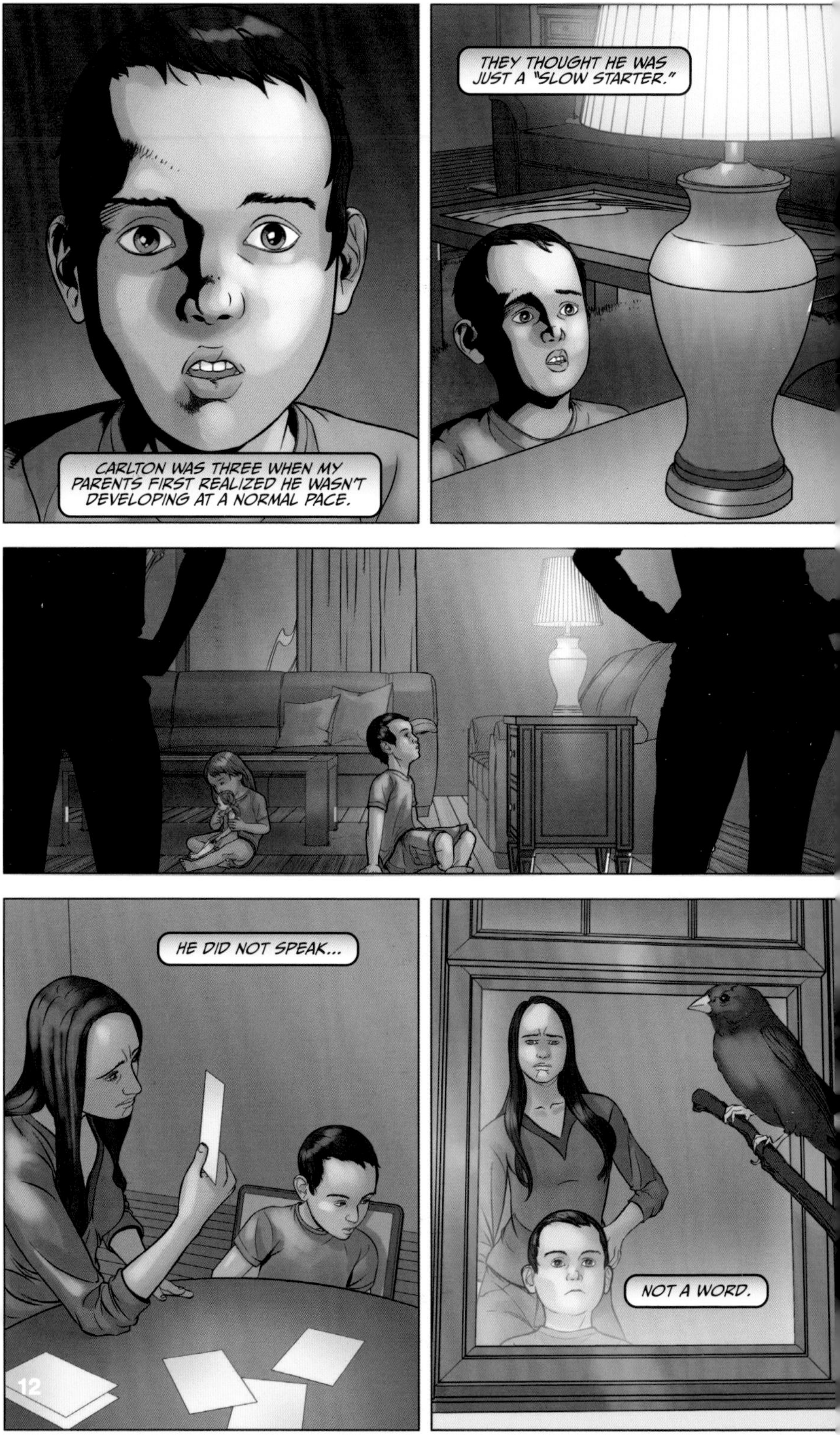
CARLTON WAS THREE WHEN MY PARENTS FIRST REALIZED HE WASN'T DEVELOPING AT A NORMAL PACE.
THEY THOUGHT HE WAS JUST A "SLOW STARTER."
HE DID NOT SPEAK...
NOT A WORD.

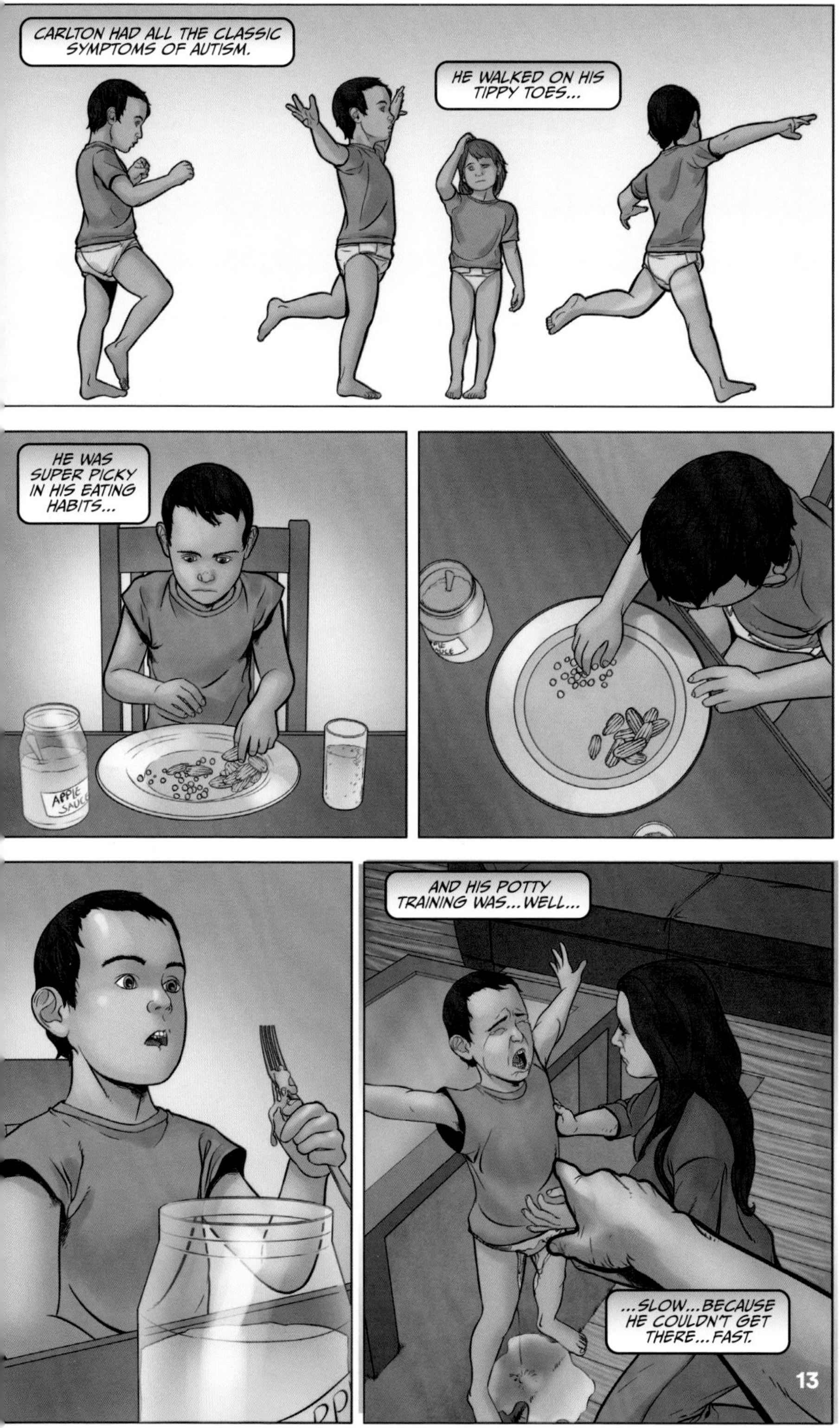
CARLTON HAD ALL THE CLASSIC SYMPTOMS OF AUTISM.
HE WALKED ON HIS TIPPY TOES...
HE WAS SUPER PICKY IN HIS EATING HABITS...
APPLE SAUCE
AND HIS POTTY TRAINING WAS...WELL...
...SLOW...BECAUSE HE COULDN'T GET THERE...FAST.

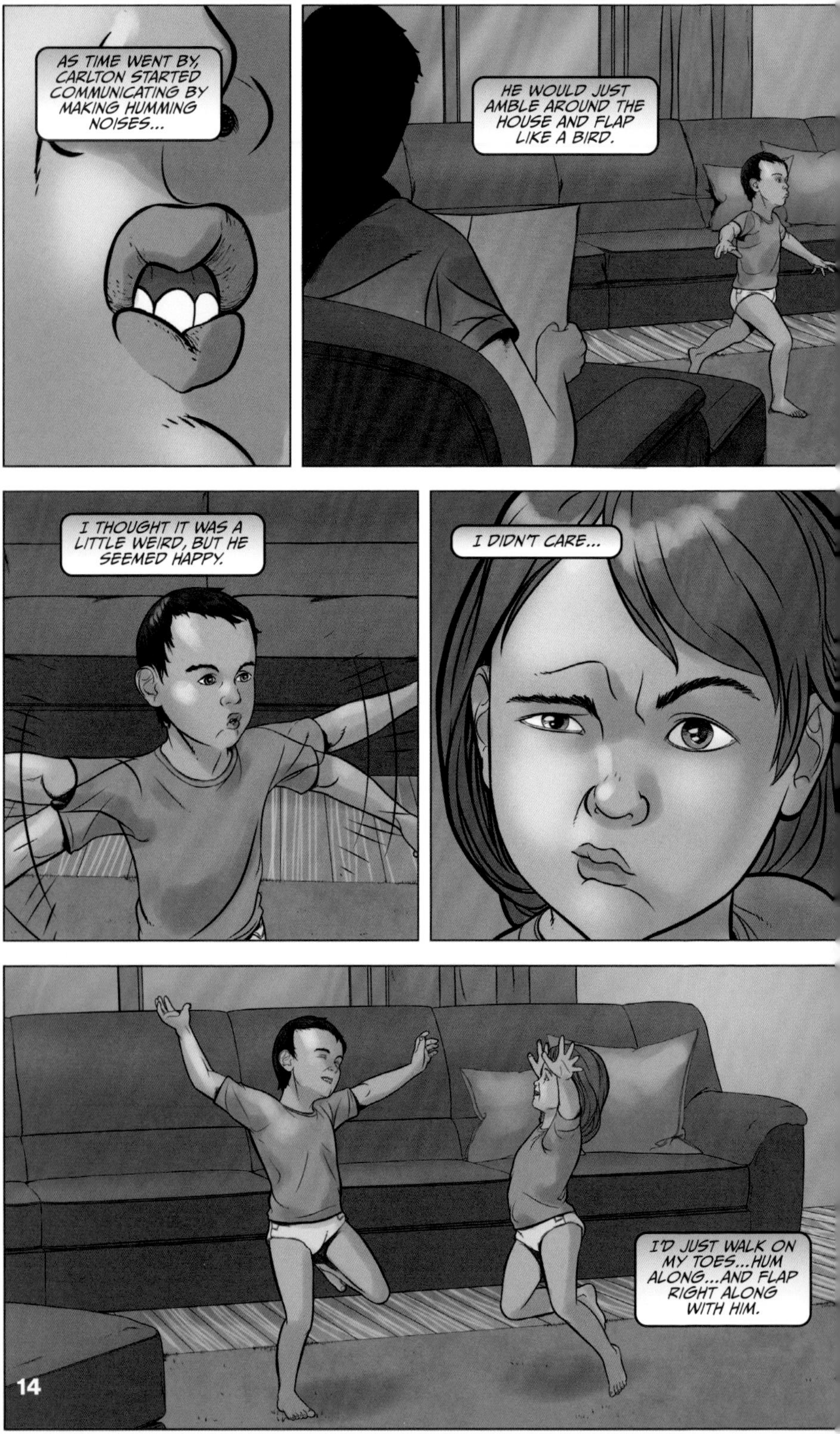
AS TIME WENT BY, CARLTON STARTED COMMUNICATING BY MAKING HUMMING NOISES...
HE WOULD JUST AMBLE AROUND THE HOUSE AND FLAP LIKE A BIRD.
I THOUGHT IT WAS A LITTLE WEIRD, BUT HE SEEMED HAPPY.
I DIDN'T CARE...
I'D JUST WALK ON MY TOES...HUM ALONG...AND FLAP RIGHT ALONG WITH HIM.

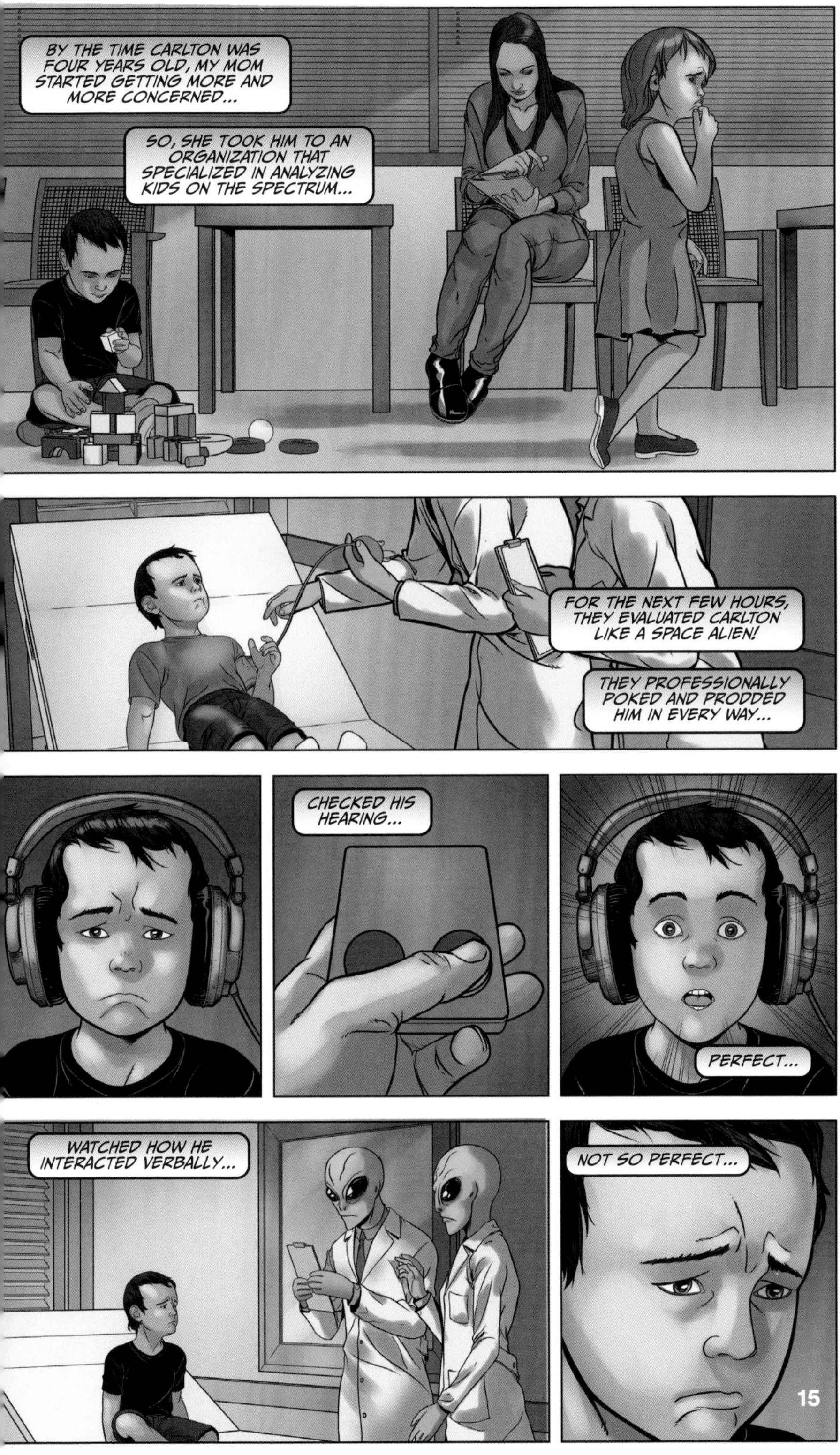

BY THE TIME CARLTON WAS FOUR YEARS OLD, MY MOM STARTED GETTING MORE AND MORE CONCERNED...
SO, SHE TOOK HIM TO AN ORGANIZATION THAT SPECIALIZED IN ANALYZING KIDS ON THE SPECTRUM...
FOR THE NEXT FEW HOURS, THEY EVALUATED CARLTON LIKE A SPACE ALIEN!
THEY PROFESSIONALLY POKED AND PRODDED HIM IN EVERY WAY...
CHECKED HIS HEARING...
PERFECT...
WATCHED HOW HE INTERACTED VERBALLY...
NOT SO PERFECT...

CARLTON WAS CLEARLY NERVOUS.

HIS HUMMING NOISES GOT LOUDER...

I THINK ALL THE MACHINES AND THE STRANGE PEOPLE IN WHITE COATS SCARED HIM...

BUT I COULDN'T DO ANYTHING TO SAVE HIM.

I JUST WATCHED HIS FACE TURN RED AS HE HELPLESSLY ROCKED BACK AND FORTH.

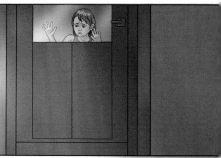

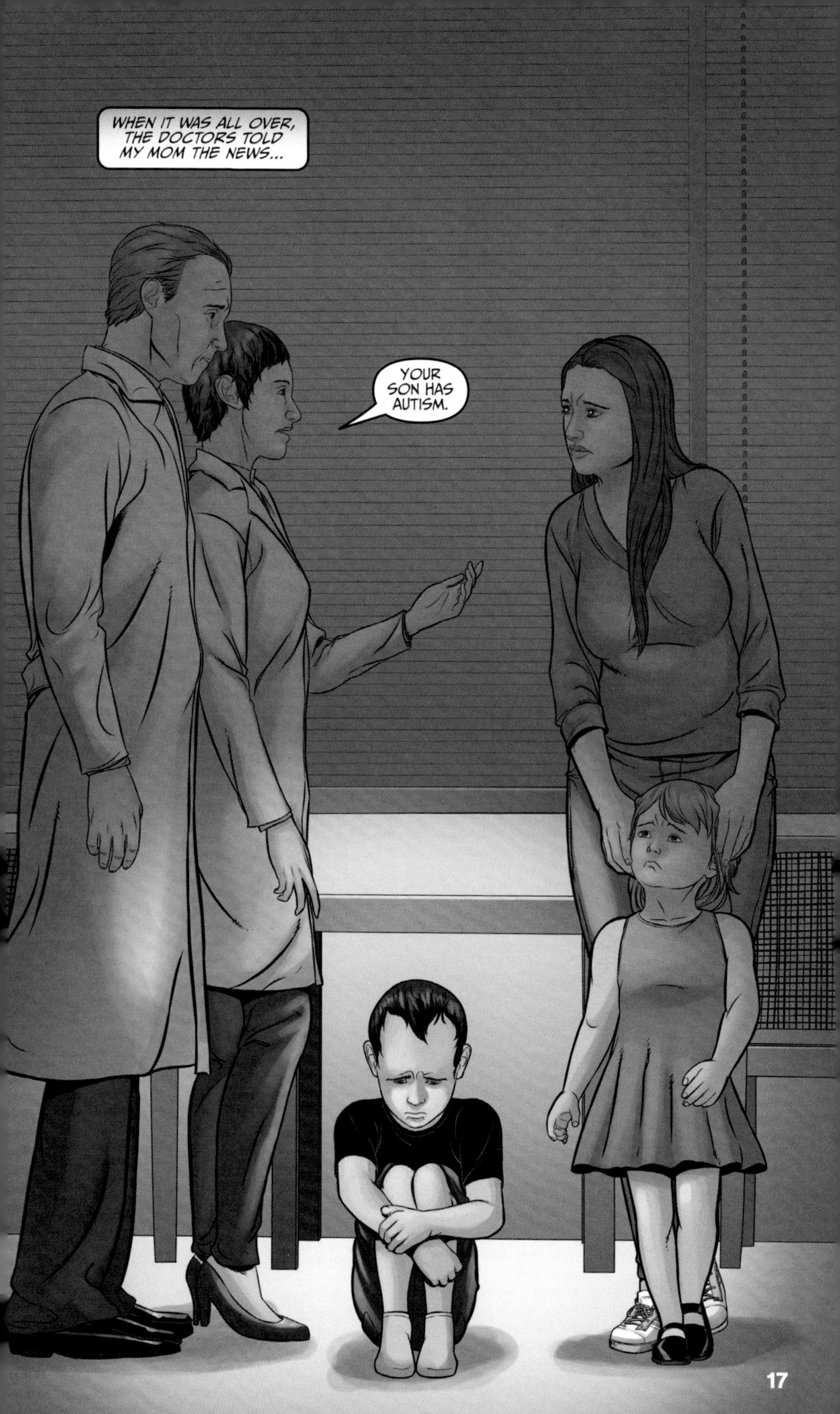
WHEN IT WAS ALL OVER, THE DOCTORS TOLD MY MOM THE NEWS...
YOUR SON HAS AUTISM.

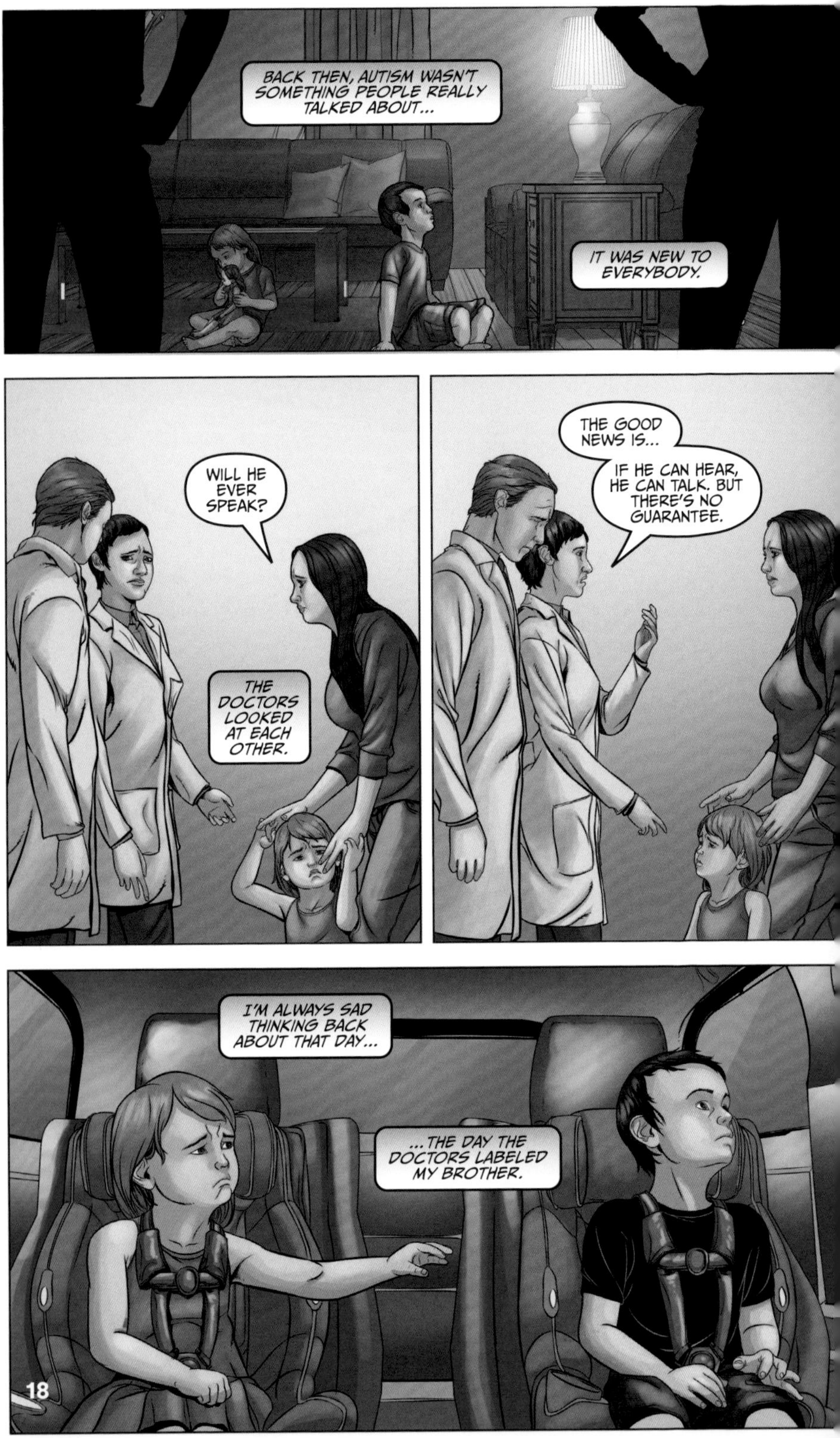

BACK THEN, AUTISM WASN'T SOMETHING PEOPLE REALLY TALKED ABOUT...
IT WAS NEW TO EVERYBODY.
WILL HE EVER SPEAK?
THE DOCTORS LOOKED AT EACH OTHER.
THE GOOD NEWS IS...
IF HE CAN HEAR, HE CAN TALK. BUT THERE'S NO GUARANTEE.
I'M ALWAYS SAD THINKING BACK ABOUT THAT DAY...
...THE DAY THE DOCTORS LABELED MY BROTHER.

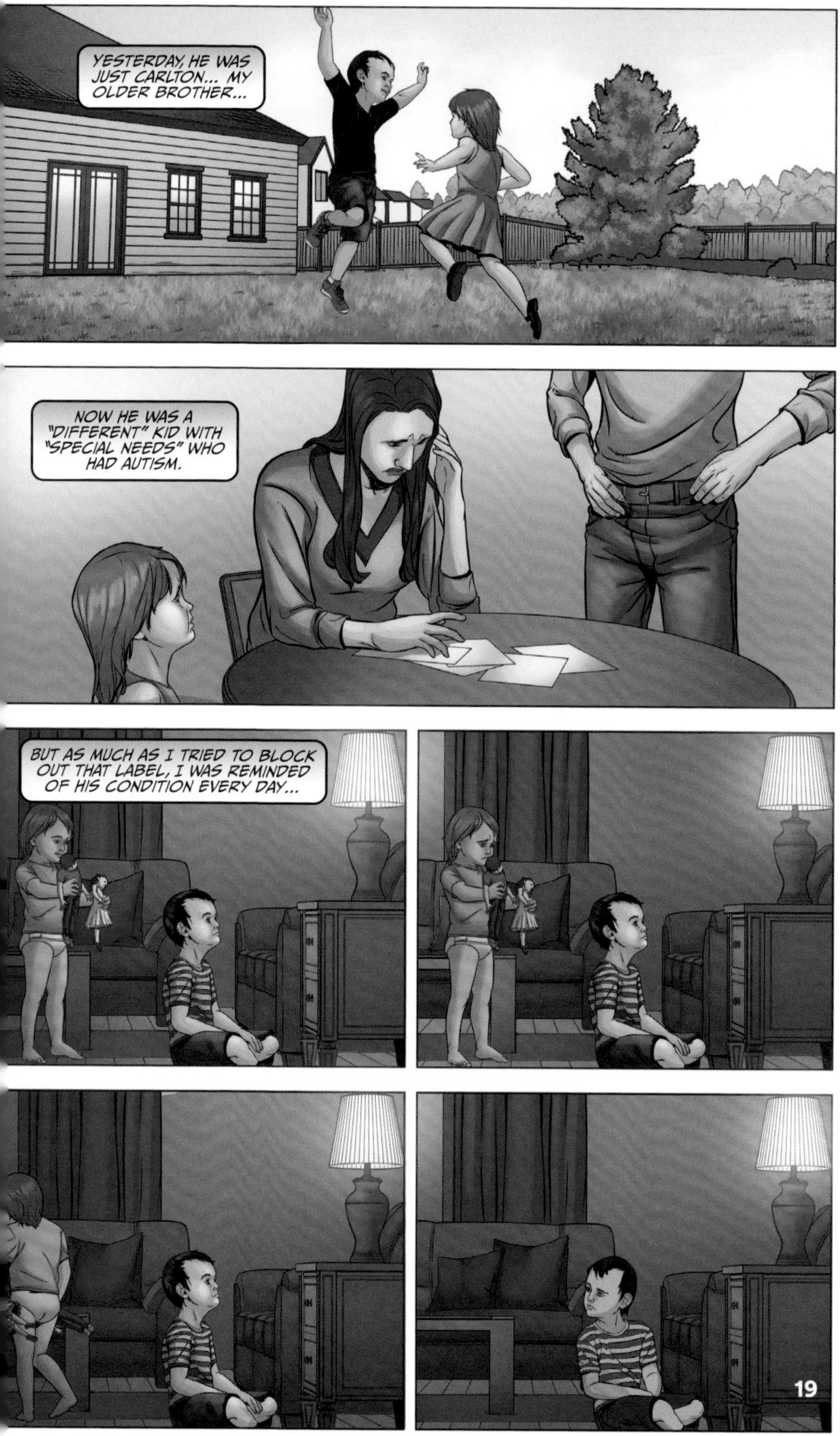
YESTERDAY, HE WAS JUST CARLTON... MY OLDER BROTHER...
NOW HE WAS A "DIFFERENT" KID WITH "SPECIAL NEEDS" WHO HAD AUTISM.
BUT AS MUCH AS I TRIED TO BLOCK OUT THAT LABEL, I WAS REMINDED OF HIS CONDITION EVERY DAY...

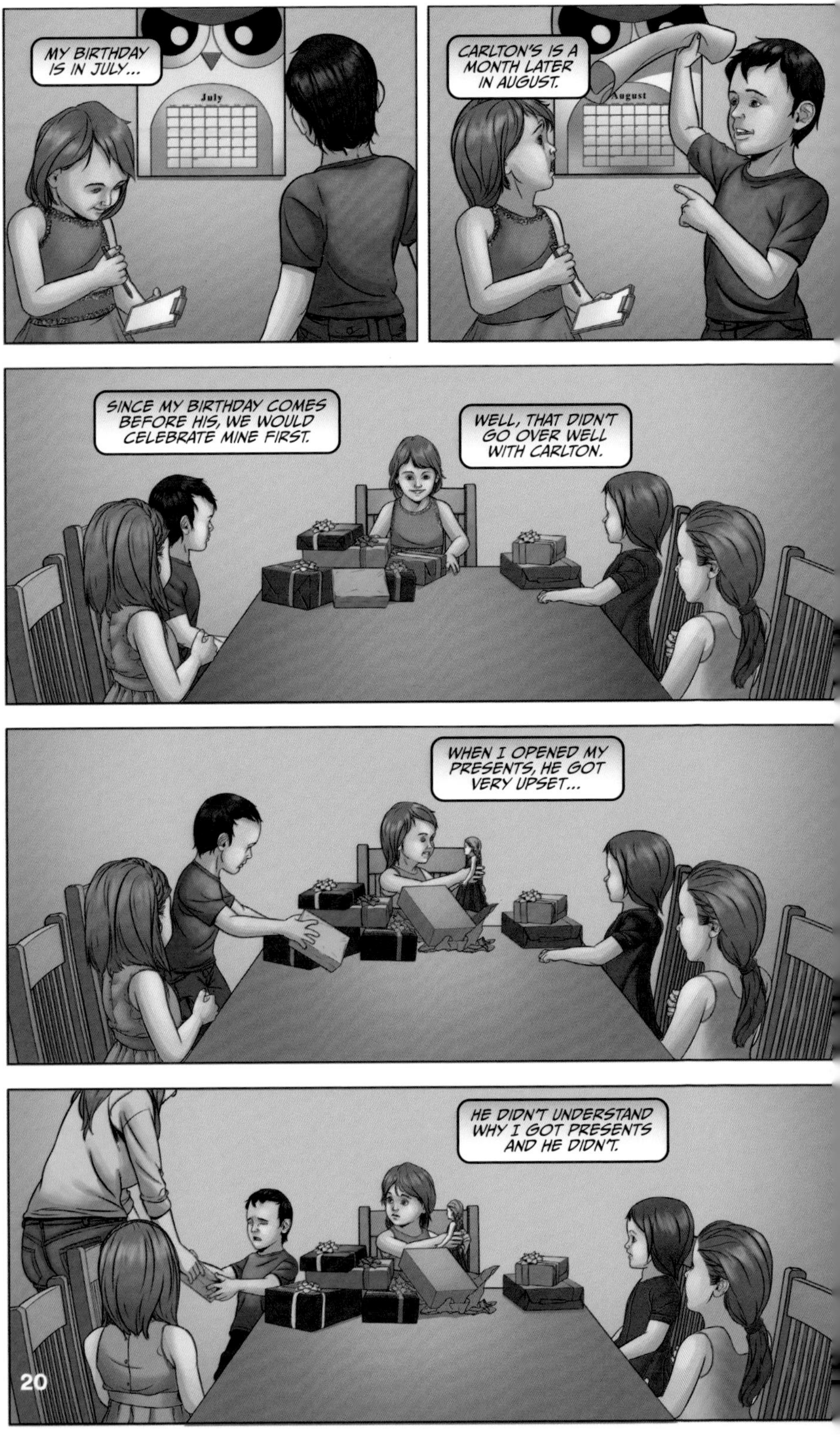
MY BIRTHDAY IS IN JULY...
July
CARLTON'S IS A MONTH LATER IN AUGUST.
August
SINCE MY BIRTHDAY COMES BEFORE HIS, WE WOULD CELEBRATE MINE FIRST.
WELL, THAT DIDN'T GO OVER WELL WITH CARLTON.
WHEN I OPENED MY PRESENTS, HE GOT VERY UPSET...
HE DIDN'T UNDERSTAND WHY I GOT PRESENTS AND HE DIDN'T.

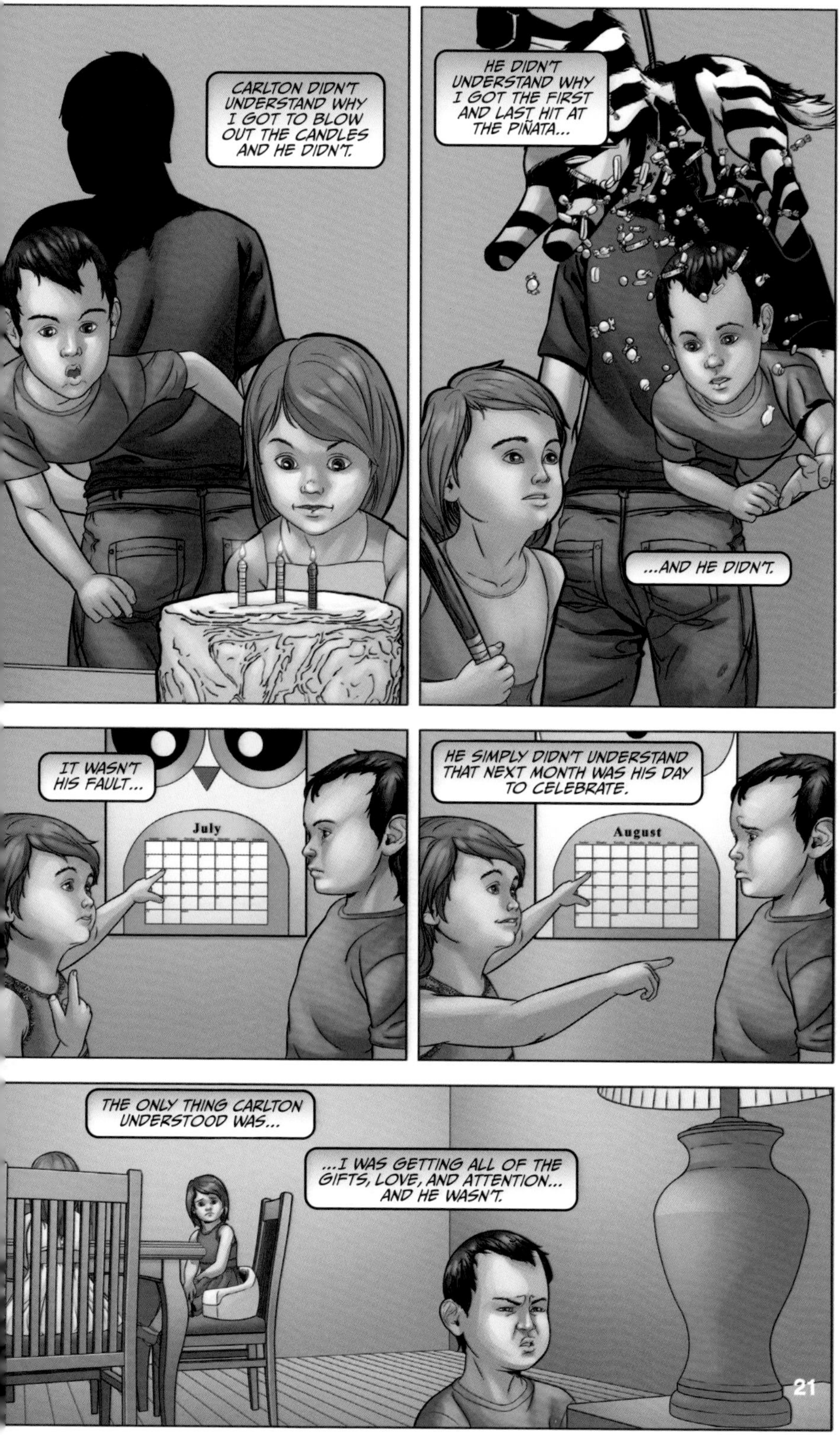
CARLTON DIDN'T UNDERSTAND WHY I GOT TO BLOW OUT THE CANDLES AND HE DIDN'T.
HE DIDN'T UNDERSTAND WHY I GOT THE FIRST AND LAST HIT AT THE PIÑATA...
...AND HE DIDN'T.
IT WASN'T HIS FAULT...
July
HE SIMPLY DIDN'T UNDERSTAND THAT NEXT MONTH WAS HIS DAY TO CELEBRATE.
August
THE ONLY THING CARLTON UNDERSTOOD WAS...
...I WAS GETTING ALL OF THE GIFTS, LOVE, AND ATTENTION... AND HE WASN'T.

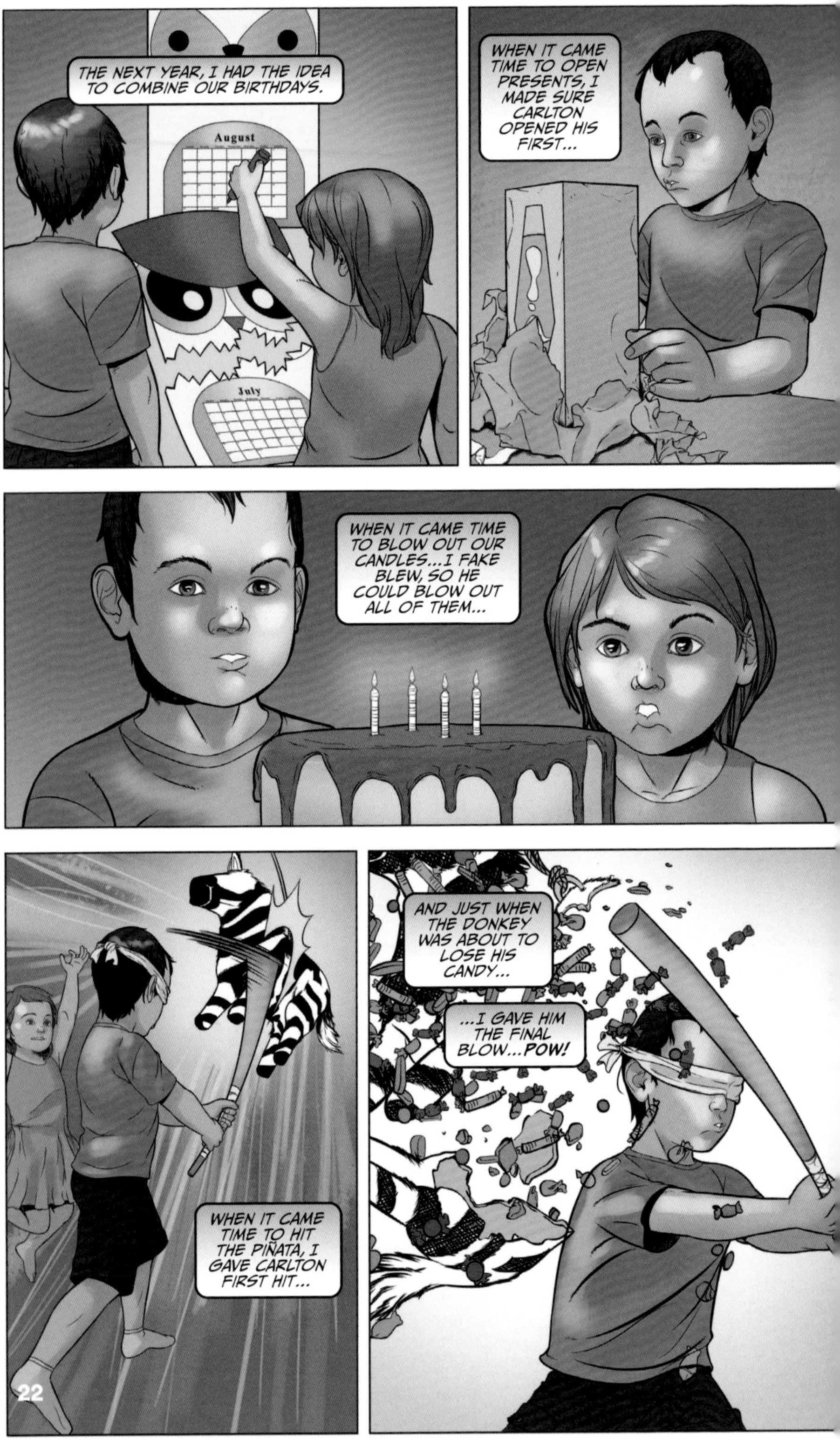
THE NEXT YEAR, I HAD THE IDEA TO COMBINE OUR BIRTHDAYS.
August
July
WHEN IT CAME TIME TO OPEN PRESENTS, I MADE SURE CARLTON OPENED HIS FIRST...
WHEN IT CAME TIME TO BLOW OUT OUR CANDLES...I FAKE BLEW, SO HE COULD BLOW OUT ALL OF THEM...
WHEN IT CAME TIME TO HIT THE PIÑATA, I GAVE CARLTON FIRST HIT...
AND JUST WHEN THE DONKEY WAS ABOUT TO LOSE HIS CANDY...
...I GAVE HIM THE FINAL BLOW...**POW!**

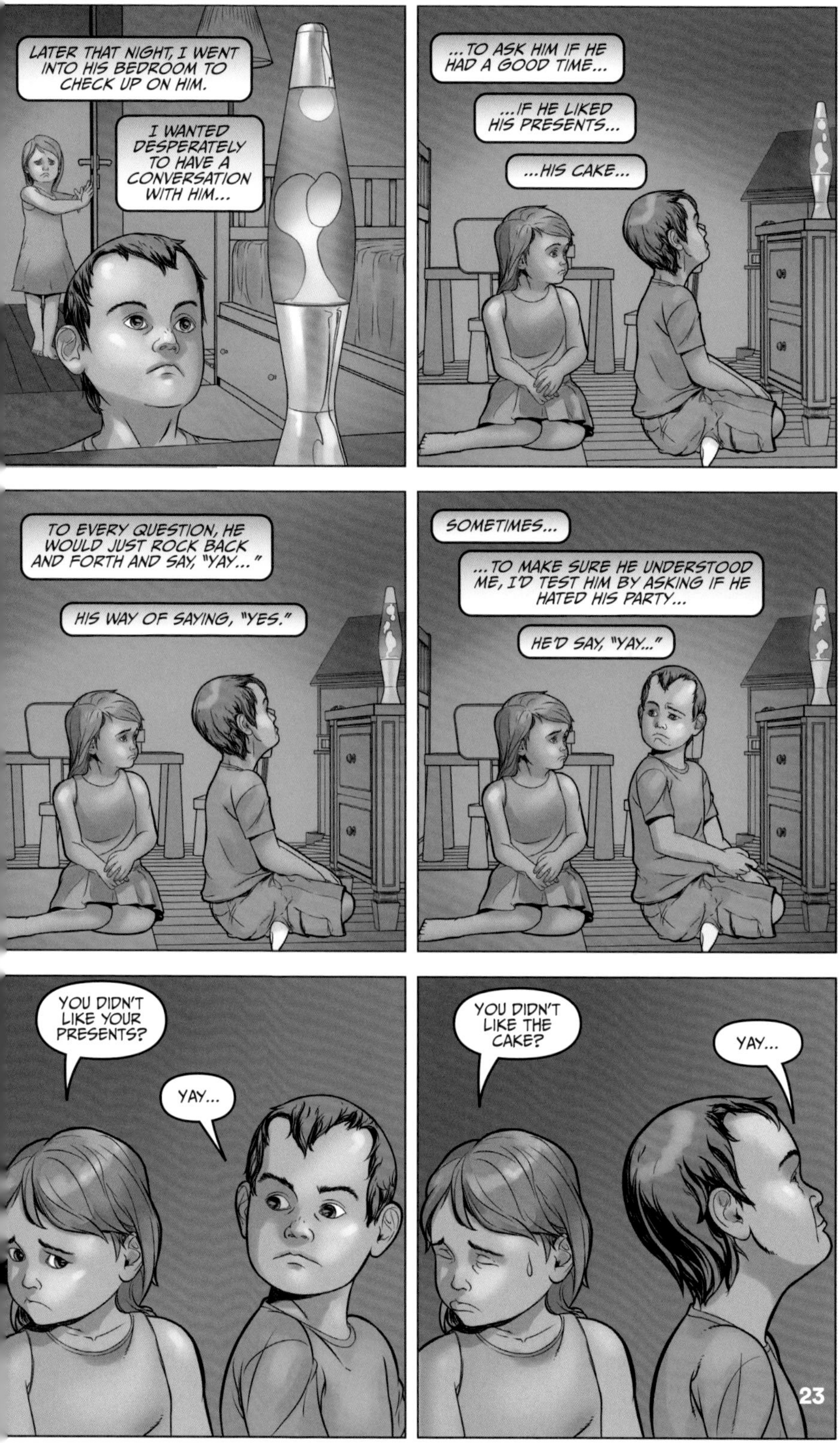
LATER THAT NIGHT, I WENT INTO HIS BEDROOM TO CHECK UP ON HIM.
I WANTED DESPERATELY TO HAVE A CONVERSATION WITH HIM...
...TO ASK HIM IF HE HAD A GOOD TIME...
...IF HE LIKED HIS PRESENTS...
...HIS CAKE...
TO EVERY QUESTION, HE WOULD JUST ROCK BACK AND FORTH AND SAY, "YAY..."
HIS WAY OF SAYING, "YES."
SOMETIMES...
...TO MAKE SURE HE UNDERSTOOD ME, I'D TEST HIM BY ASKING IF HE HATED HIS PARTY...
HE'D SAY, "YAY..."
YOU DIDN'T LIKE YOUR PRESENTS?
YAY...
YOU DIDN'T LIKE THE CAKE?
YAY...

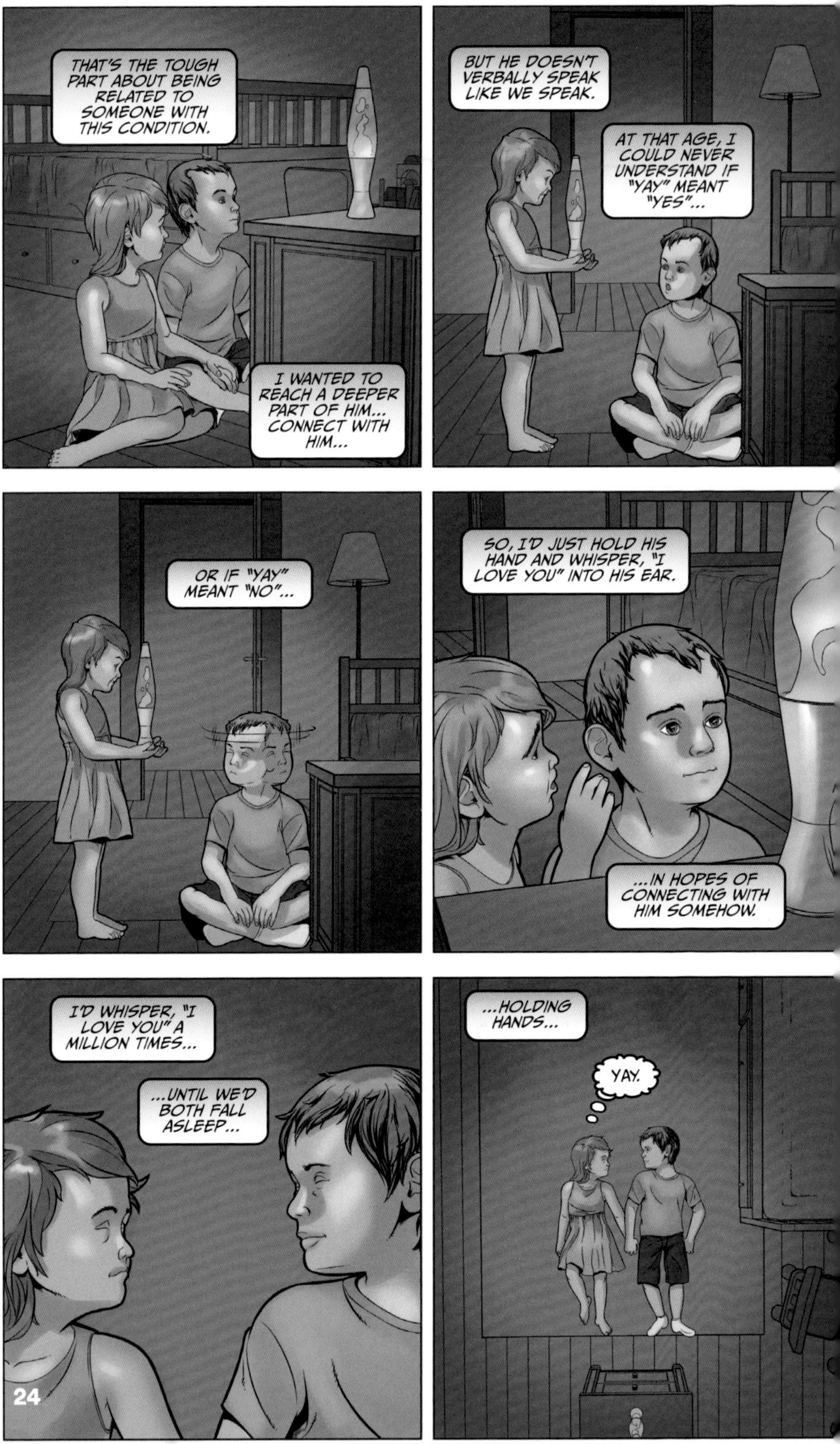
THAT'S THE TOUGH PART ABOUT BEING RELATED TO SOMEONE WITH THIS CONDITION.
I WANTED TO REACH A DEEPER PART OF HIM... CONNECT WITH HIM...
BUT HE DOESN'T VERBALLY SPEAK LIKE WE SPEAK.
AT THAT AGE, I COULD NEVER UNDERSTAND IF "YAY" MEANT "YES"...
OR IF "YAY" MEANT "NO"...
SO, I'D JUST HOLD HIS HAND AND WHISPER, "I LOVE YOU" INTO HIS EAR.
...IN HOPES OF CONNECTING WITH HIM SOMEHOW.
I'D WHISPER, "I LOVE YOU" A MILLION TIMES...
...UNTIL WE'D BOTH FALL ASLEEP...
...HOLDING HANDS...
YAY.

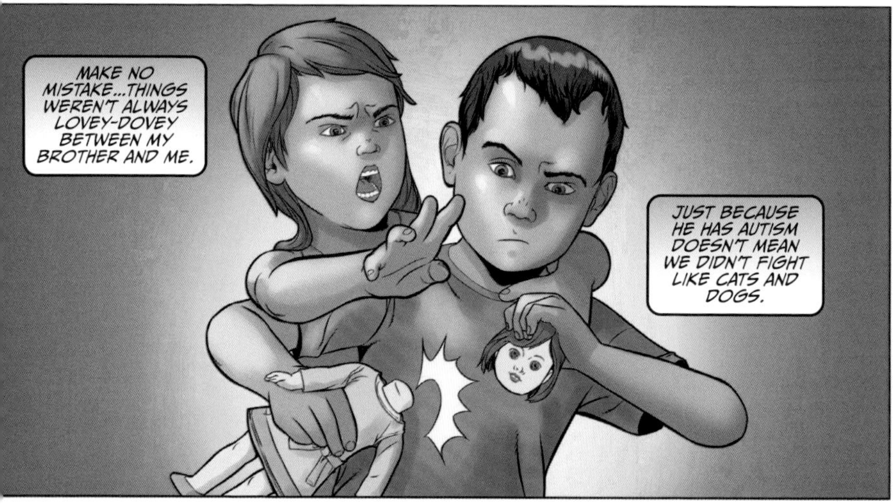
MAKE NO MISTAKE...THINGS WEREN'T ALWAYS LOVEY-DOVEY BETWEEN MY BROTHER AND ME.
JUST BECAUSE HE HAS AUTISM DOESN'T MEAN WE DIDN'T FIGHT LIKE CATS AND DOGS.

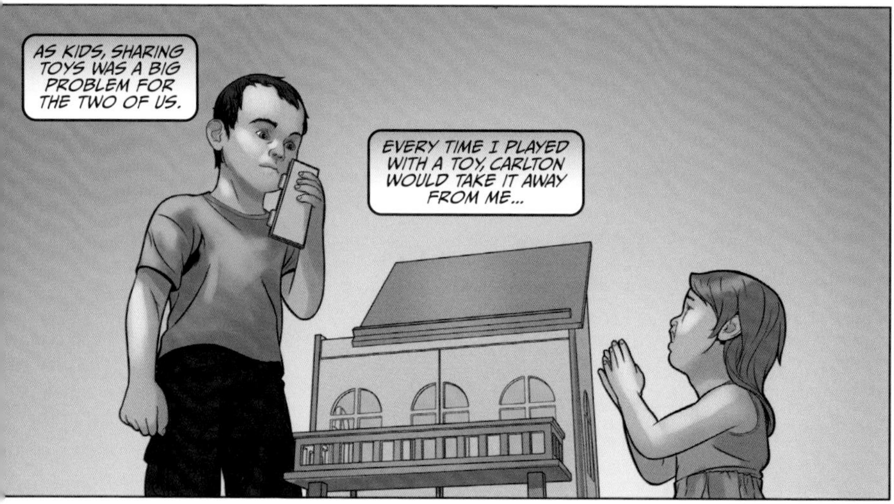
AS KIDS, SHARING TOYS WAS A BIG PROBLEM FOR THE TWO OF US.
EVERY TIME I PLAYED WITH A TOY, CARLTON WOULD TAKE IT AWAY FROM ME...

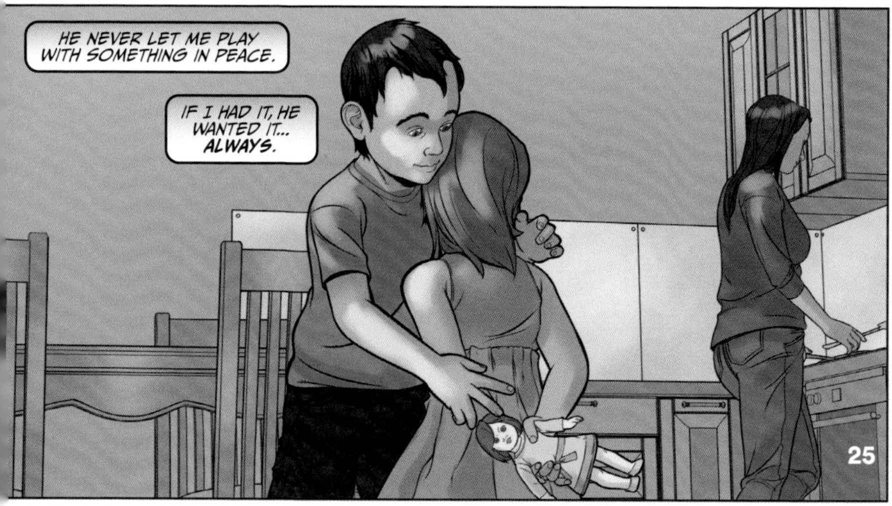
HE NEVER LET ME PLAY WITH SOMETHING IN PEACE.
IF I HAD IT, HE WANTED IT... **ALWAYS.**

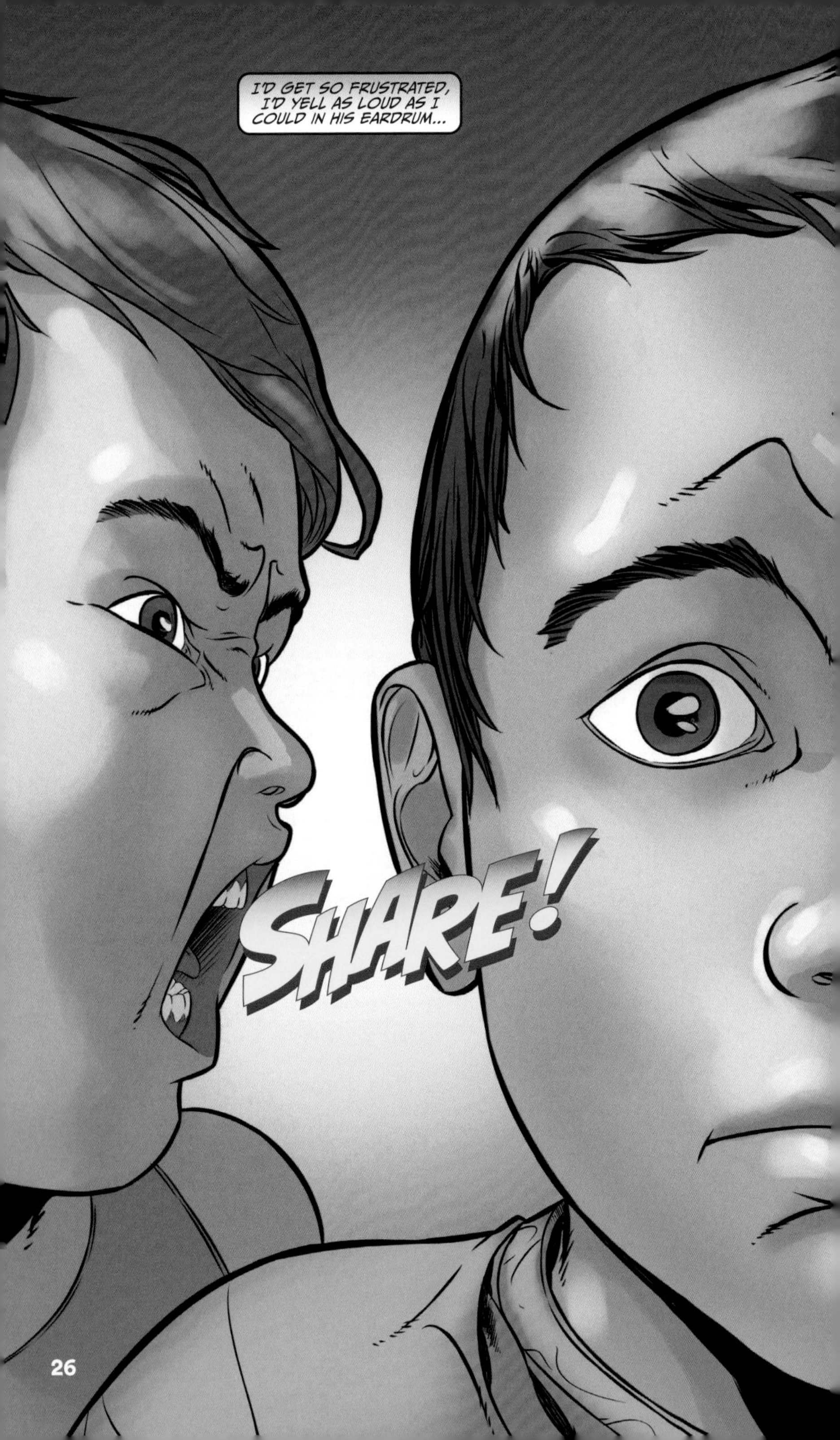
I'D GET SO FRUSTRATED, I'D YELL AS LOUD AS I COULD IN HIS EARDRUM...
SHARE!

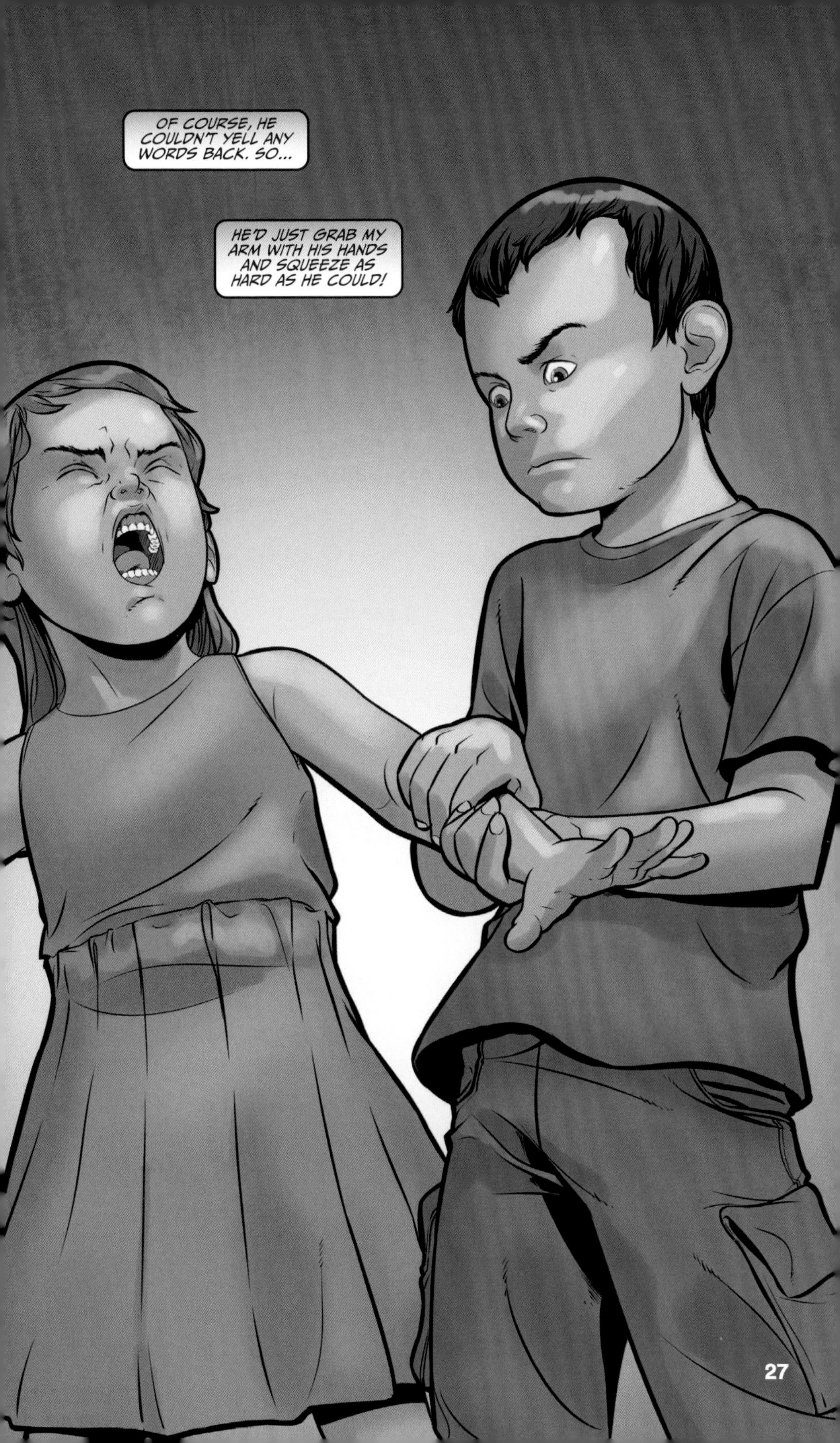
OF COURSE, HE COULDN'T YELL ANY WORDS BACK. SO...
HE'D JUST GRAB MY ARM WITH HIS HANDS AND SQUEEZE AS HARD AS HE COULD!

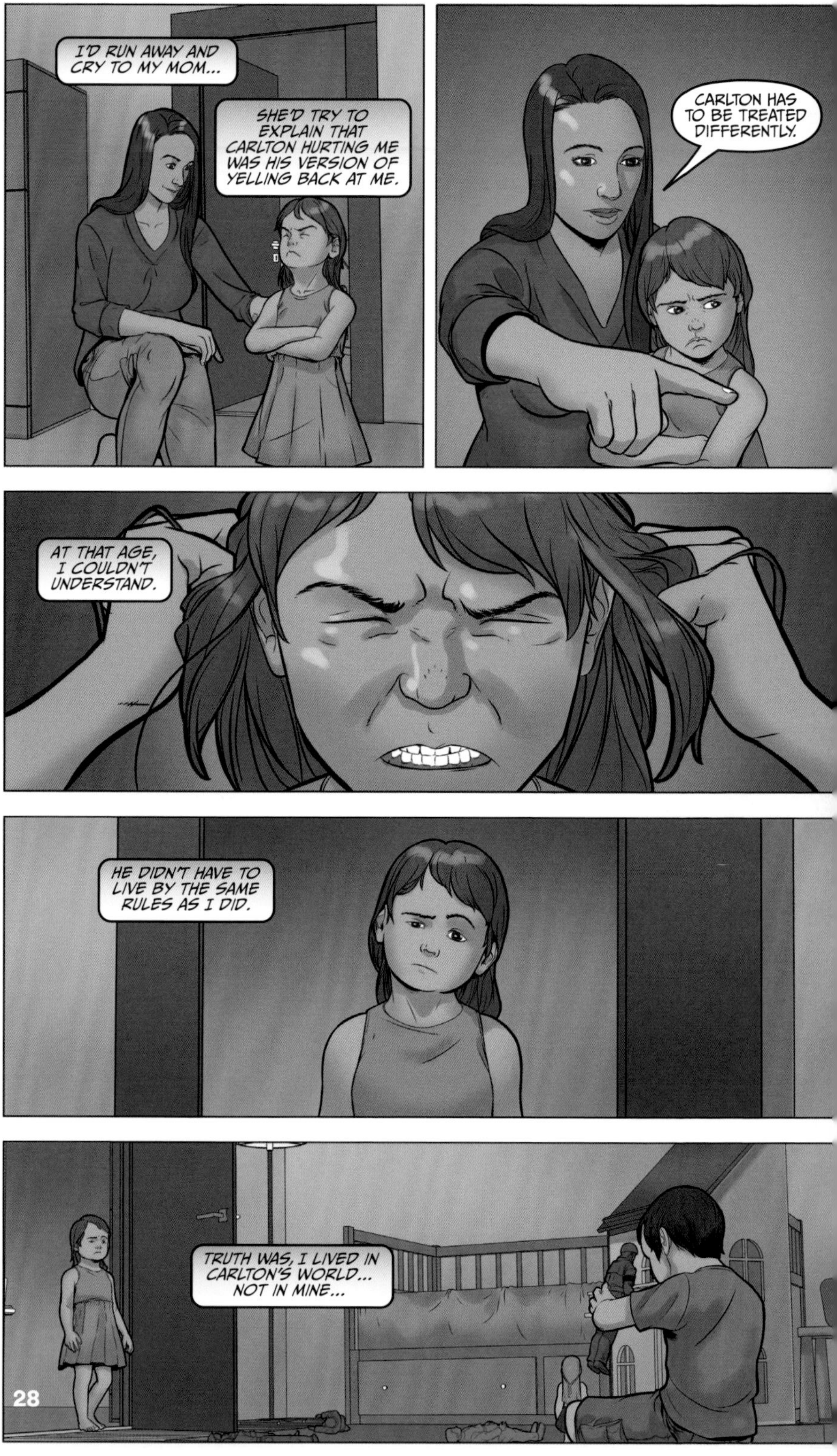
I'D RUN AWAY AND CRY TO MY MOM...
SHE'D TRY TO EXPLAIN THAT CARLTON HURTING ME WAS HIS VERSION OF YELLING BACK AT ME.
CARLTON HAS TO BE TREATED DIFFERENTLY.
AT THAT AGE, I COULDN'T UNDERSTAND.
HE DIDN'T HAVE TO LIVE BY THE SAME RULES AS I DID.
TRUTH WAS, I LIVED IN CARLTON'S WORLD... NOT IN MINE...

AND IF I WAS GOING TO BOND WITH HIM AND TRULY UNDERSTAND HIM...

I HAD TO TAKE THE GOOD WITH THE BAD...

...NO MATTER HOW BAD THE BAD WAS.

...NO MATTER HOW IT MADE ME FEEL.

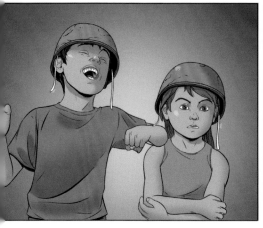

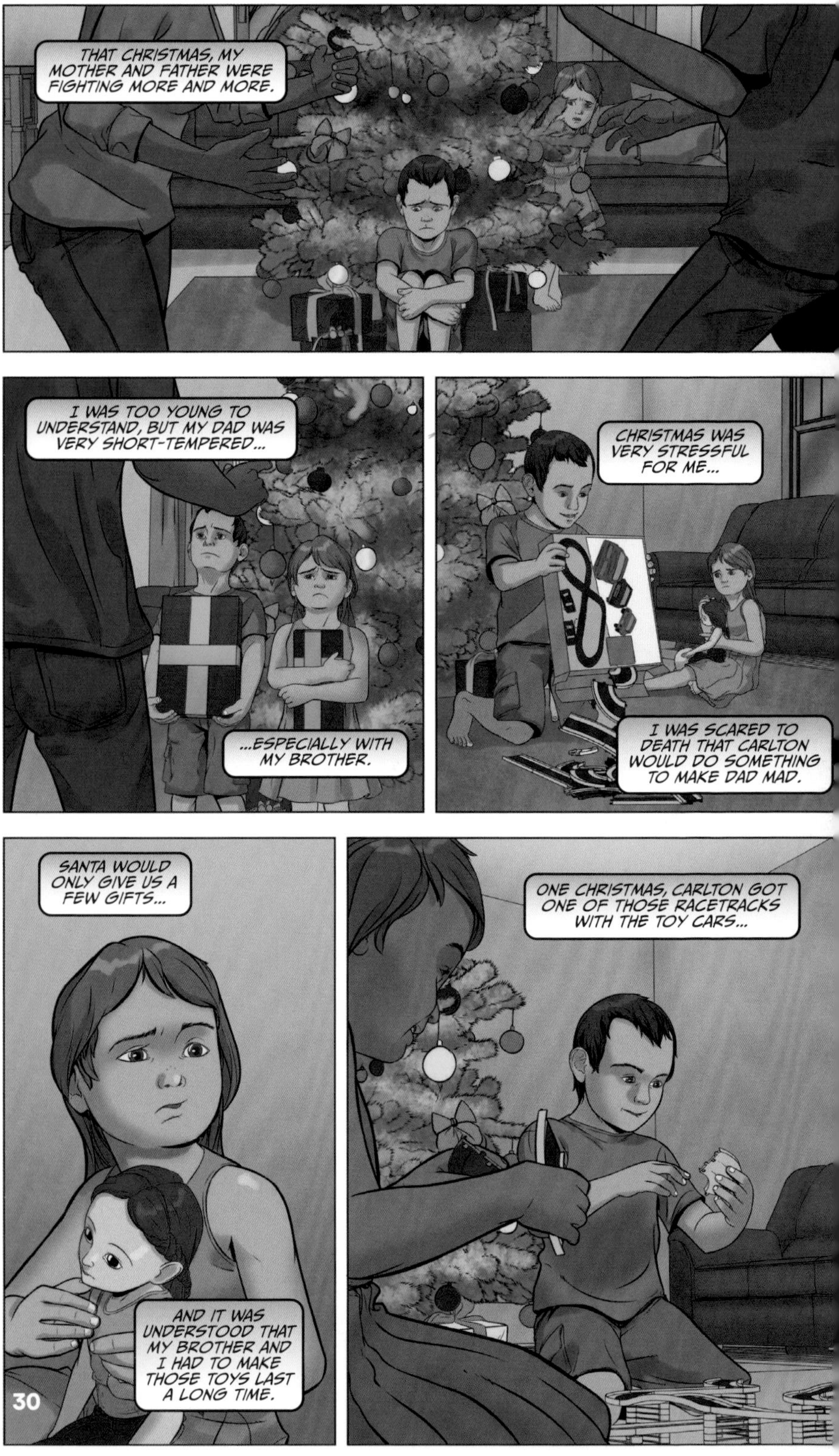
THAT CHRISTMAS, MY MOTHER AND FATHER WERE FIGHTING MORE AND MORE.
I WAS TOO YOUNG TO UNDERSTAND, BUT MY DAD WAS VERY SHORT-TEMPERED...
...ESPECIALLY WITH MY BROTHER.
CHRISTMAS WAS VERY STRESSFUL FOR ME...
I WAS SCARED TO DEATH THAT CARLTON WOULD DO SOMETHING TO MAKE DAD MAD.
SANTA WOULD ONLY GIVE US A FEW GIFTS...
AND IT WAS UNDERSTOOD THAT MY BROTHER AND I HAD TO MAKE THOSE TOYS LAST A LONG TIME.
ONE CHRISTMAS, CARLTON GOT ONE OF THOSE RACETRACKS WITH THE TOY CARS...

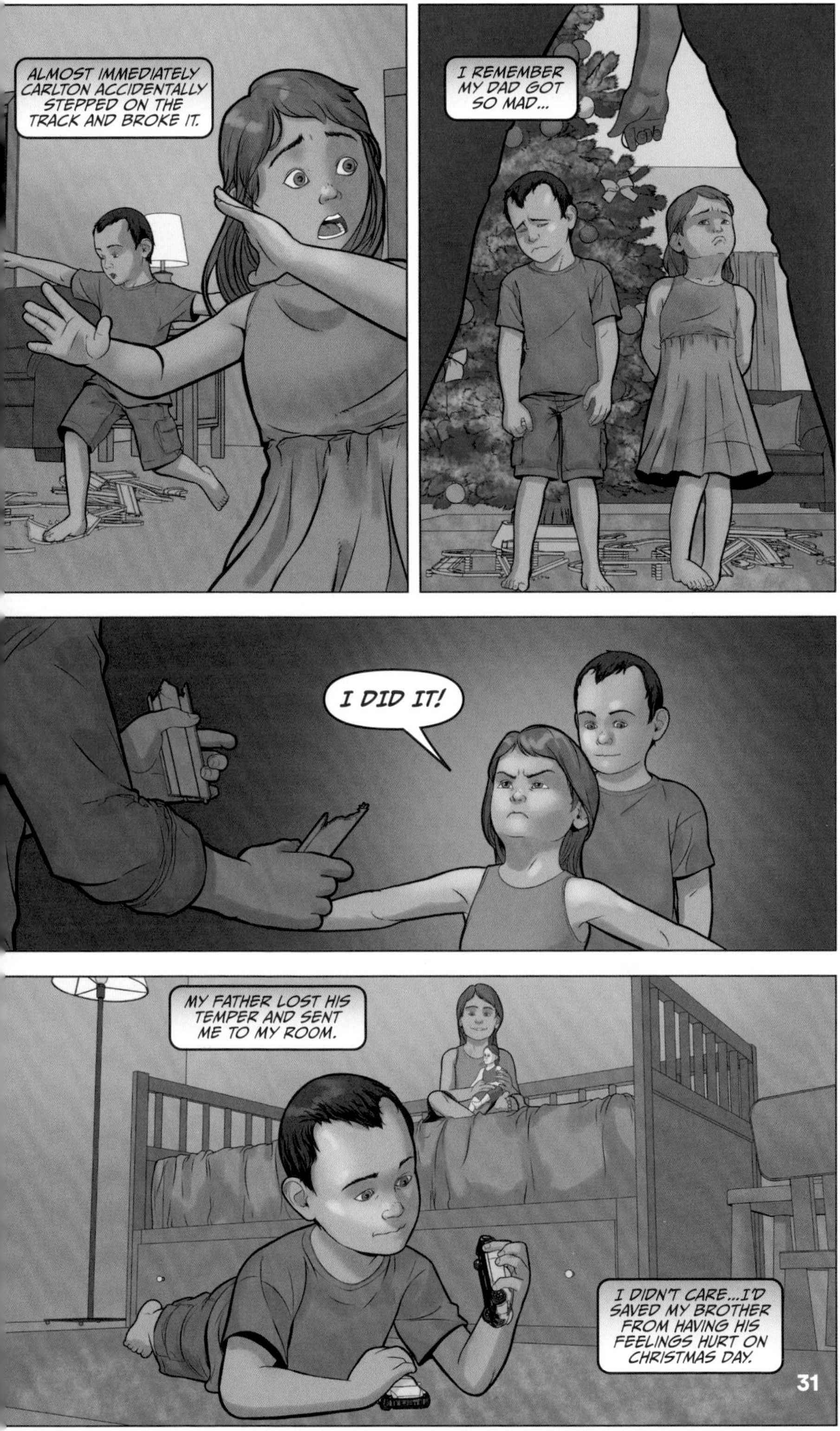

ALMOST IMMEDIATELY CARLTON ACCIDENTALLY STEPPED ON THE TRACK AND BROKE IT.
I REMEMBER MY DAD GOT SO MAD...
I DID IT!
MY FATHER LOST HIS TEMPER AND SENT ME TO MY ROOM.
I DIDN'T CARE...I'D SAVED MY BROTHER FROM HAVING HIS FEELINGS HURT ON CHRISTMAS DAY.

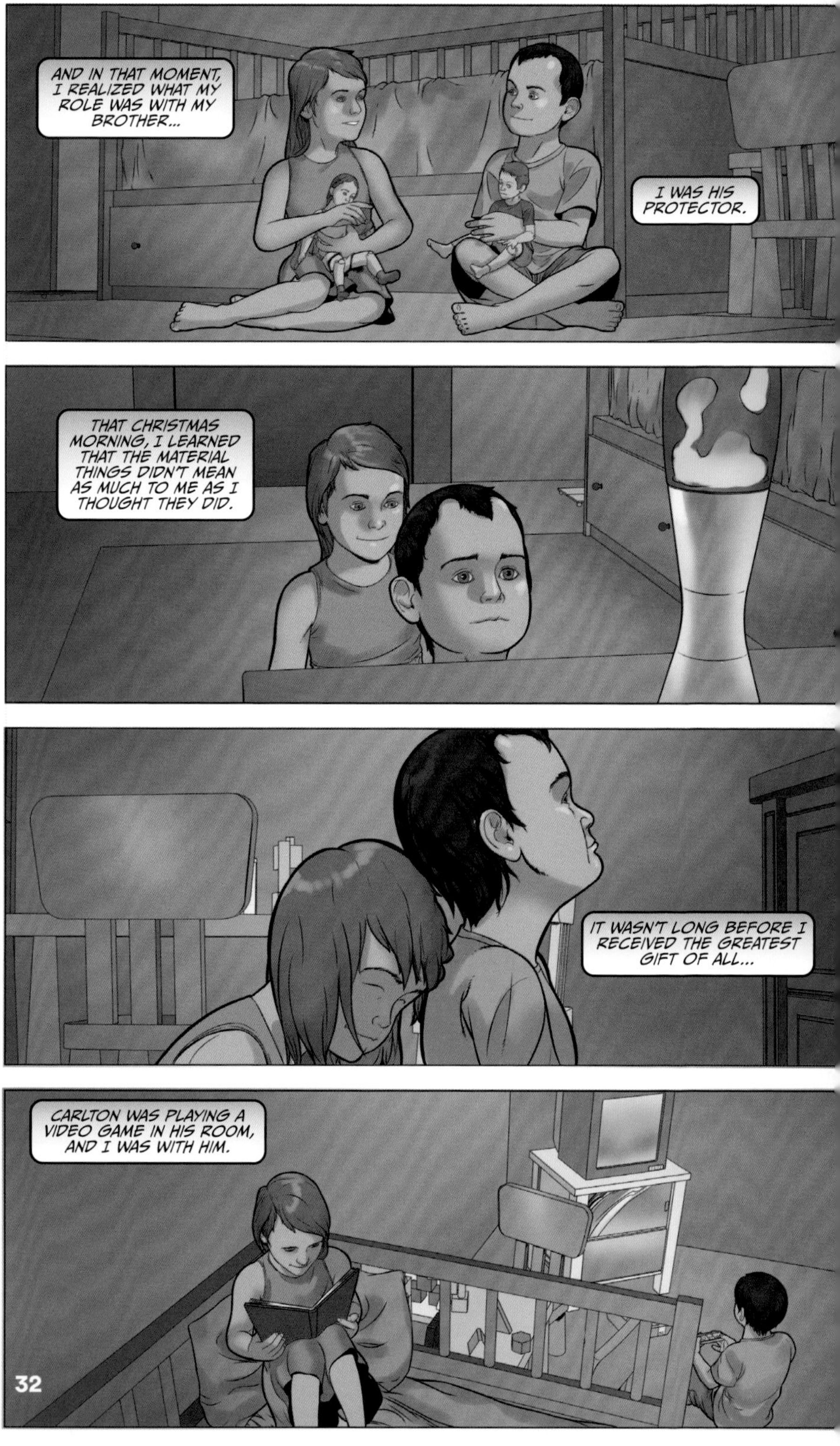
AND IN THAT MOMENT, I REALIZED WHAT MY ROLE WAS WITH MY BROTHER...
I WAS HIS PROTECTOR.
THAT CHRISTMAS MORNING, I LEARNED THAT THE MATERIAL THINGS DIDN'T MEAN AS MUCH TO ME AS I THOUGHT THEY DID.
IT WASN'T LONG BEFORE I RECEIVED THE GREATEST GIFT OF ALL...
CARLTON WAS PLAYING A VIDEO GAME IN HIS ROOM, AND I WAS WITH HIM.

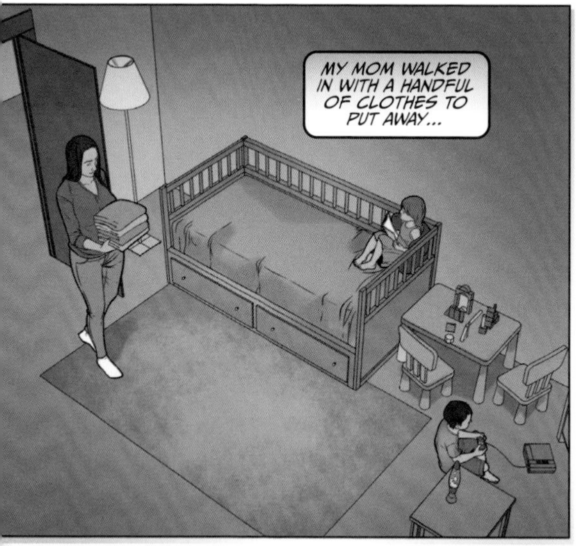
MY MOM WALKED IN WITH A HANDFUL OF CLOTHES TO PUT AWAY...

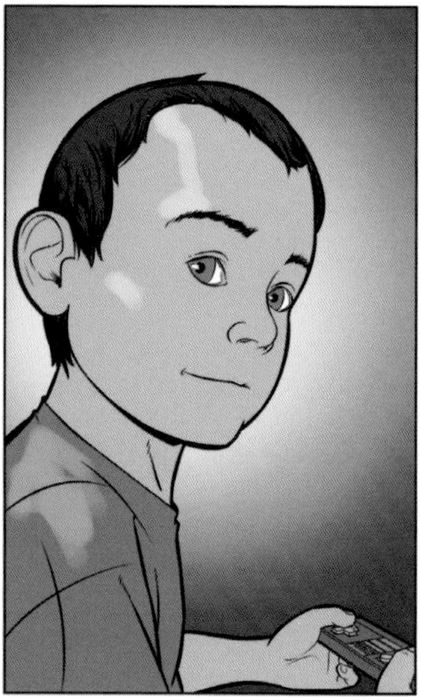

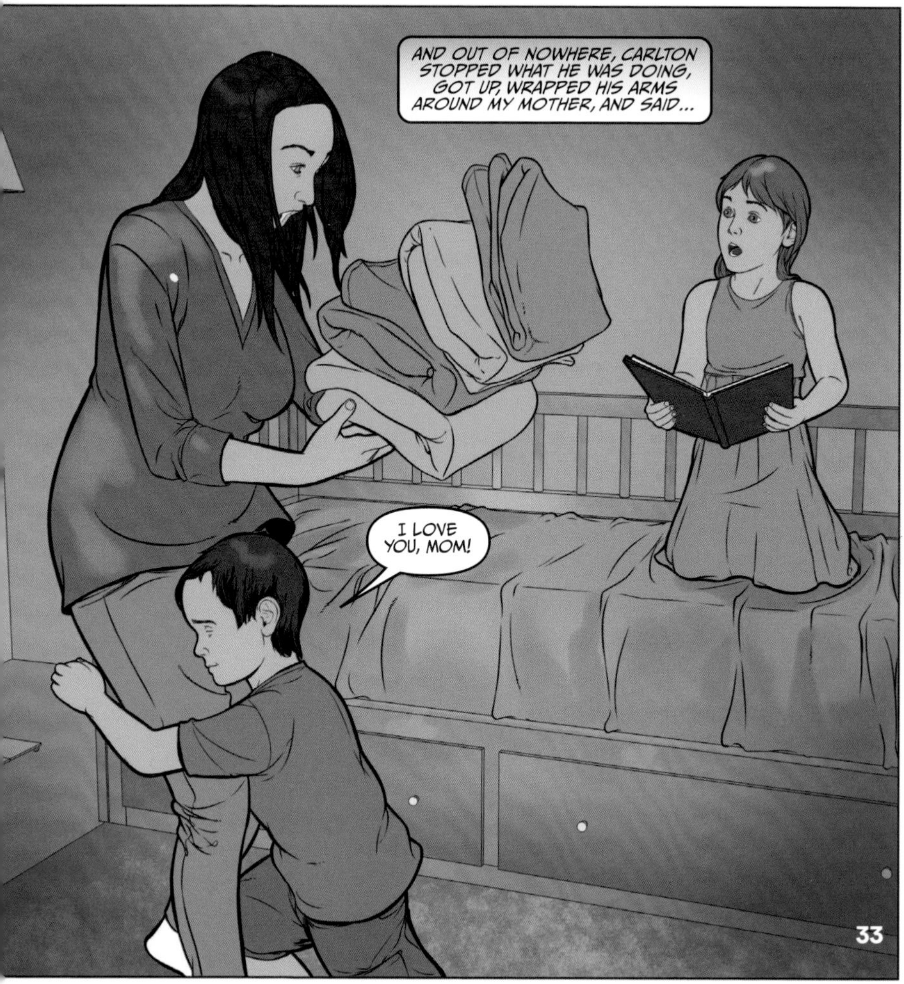
AND OUT OF NOWHERE, CARLTON STOPPED WHAT HE WAS DOING, GOT UP, WRAPPED HIS ARMS AROUND MY MOTHER, AND SAID...
I LOVE YOU, MOM!

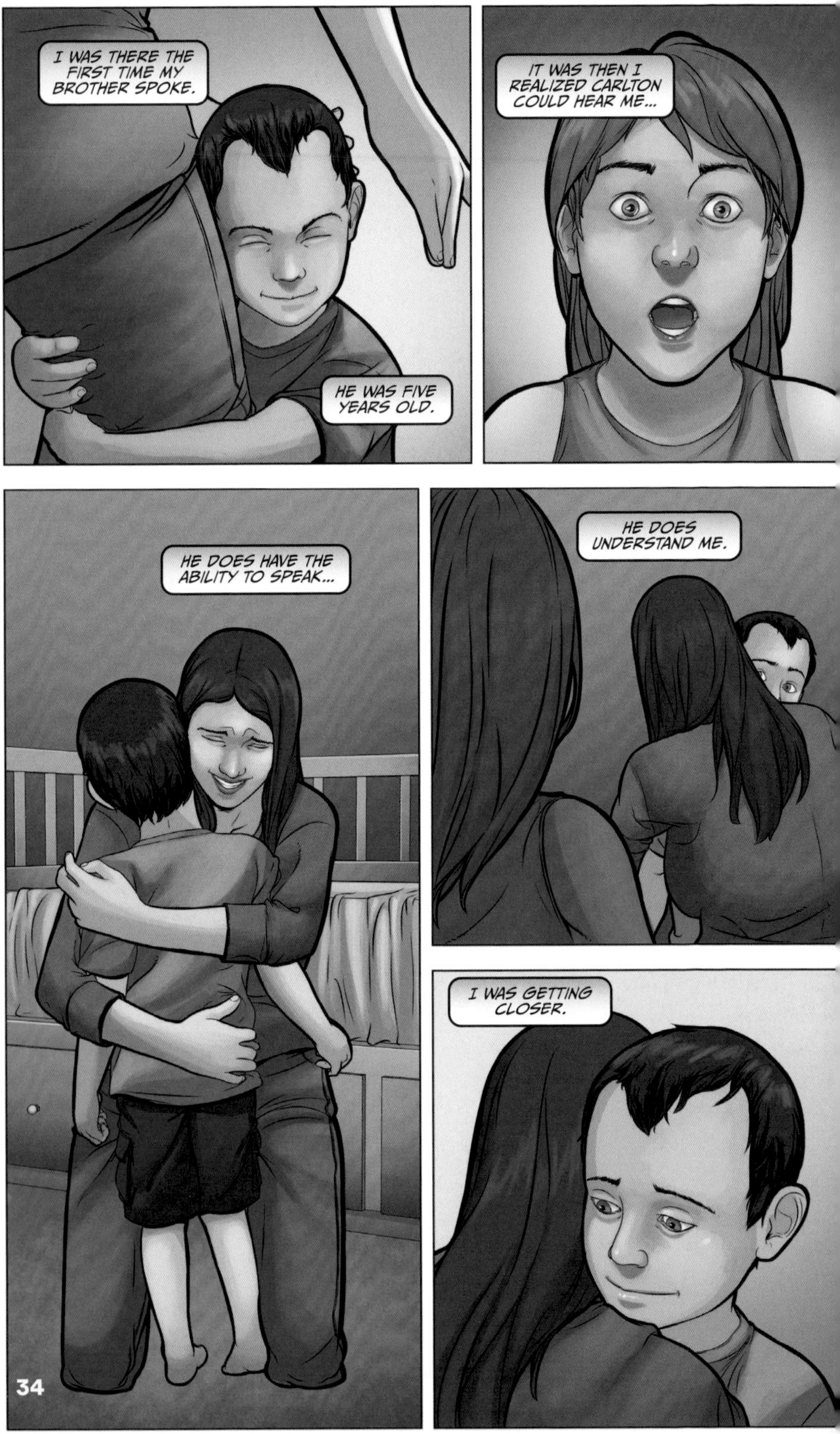
I WAS THERE THE FIRST TIME MY BROTHER SPOKE.
HE WAS FIVE YEARS OLD.
IT WAS THEN I REALIZED CARLTON COULD HEAR ME...
HE DOES HAVE THE ABILITY TO SPEAK...
HE DOES UNDERSTAND ME.
I WAS GETTING CLOSER.

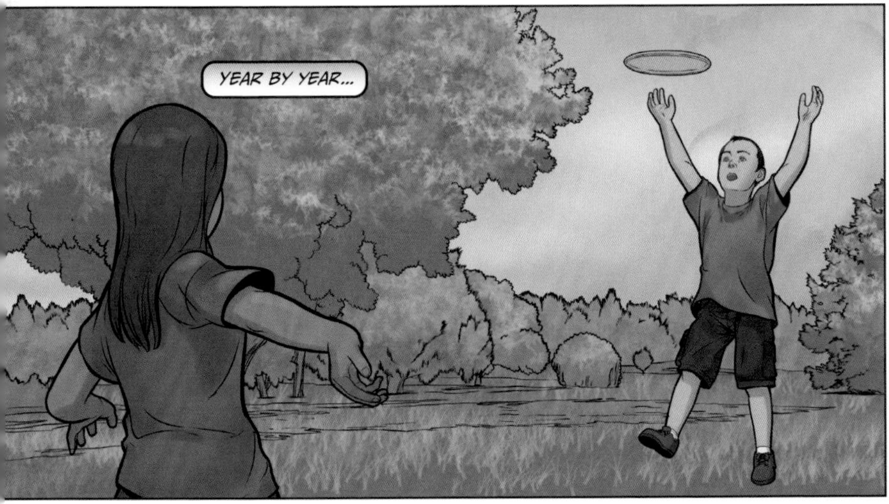
YEAR BY YEAR...

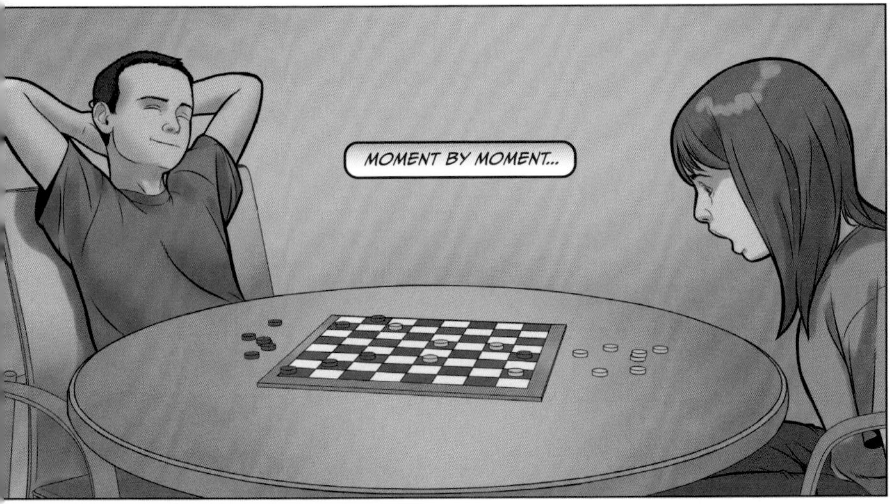
MOMENT BY MOMENT...

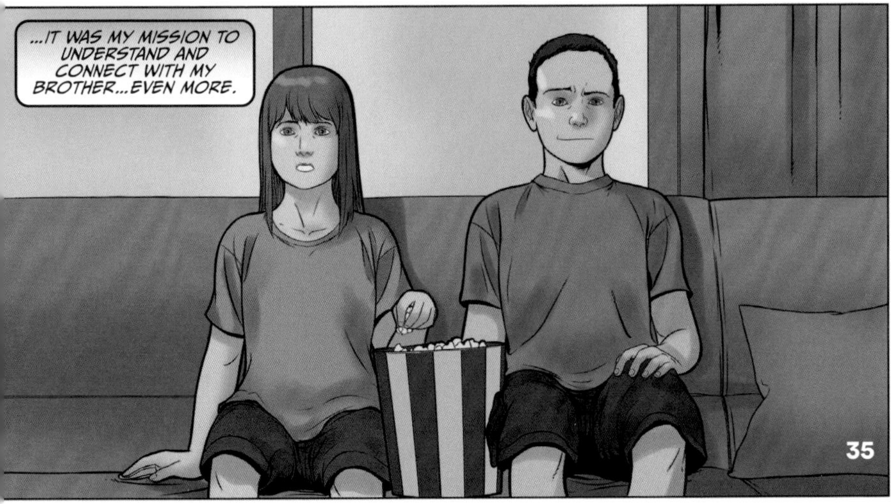
...IT WAS MY MISSION TO UNDERSTAND AND CONNECT WITH MY BROTHER...EVEN MORE.

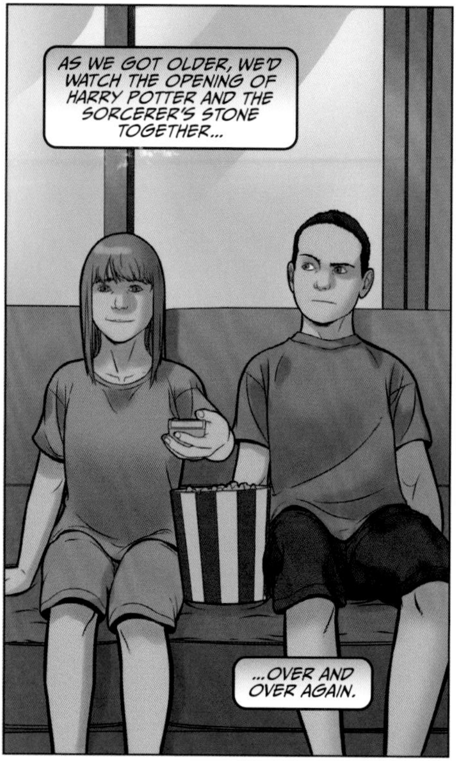
AS WE GOT OLDER, WE'D WATCH THE OPENING OF HARRY POTTER AND THE SORCERER'S STONE TOGETHER...
...OVER AND OVER AGAIN.

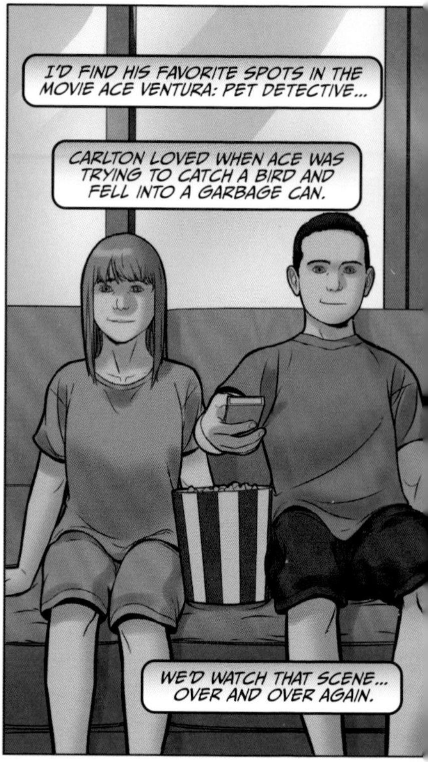
I'D FIND HIS FAVORITE SPOTS IN THE MOVIE ACE VENTURA: PET DETECTIVE...
CARLTON LOVED WHEN ACE WAS TRYING TO CATCH A BIRD AND FELL INTO A GARBAGE CAN.
WE'D WATCH THAT SCENE... OVER AND OVER AGAIN.

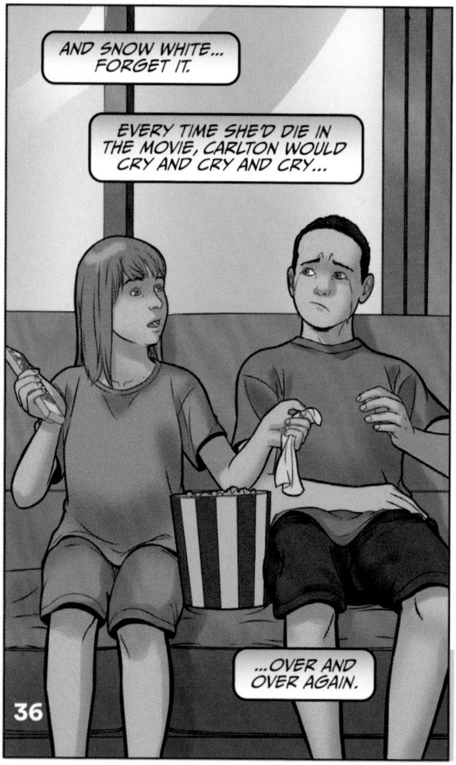
AND SNOW WHITE... FORGET IT.
EVERY TIME SHE'D DIE IN THE MOVIE, CARLTON WOULD CRY AND CRY AND CRY...
...OVER AND OVER AGAIN.

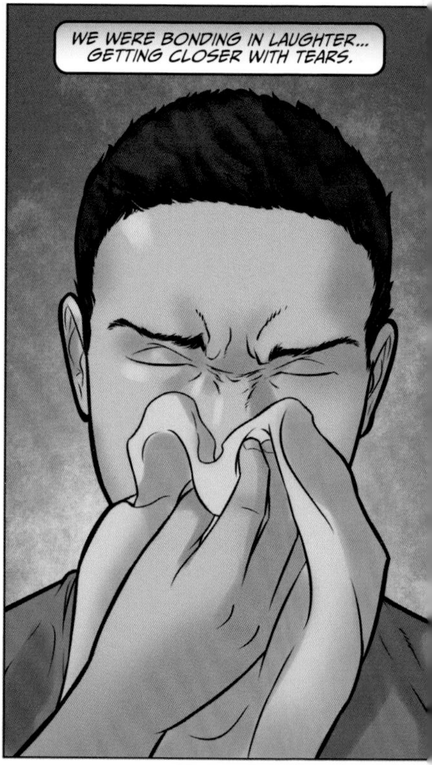
WE WERE BONDING IN LAUGHTER... GETTING CLOSER WITH TEARS.

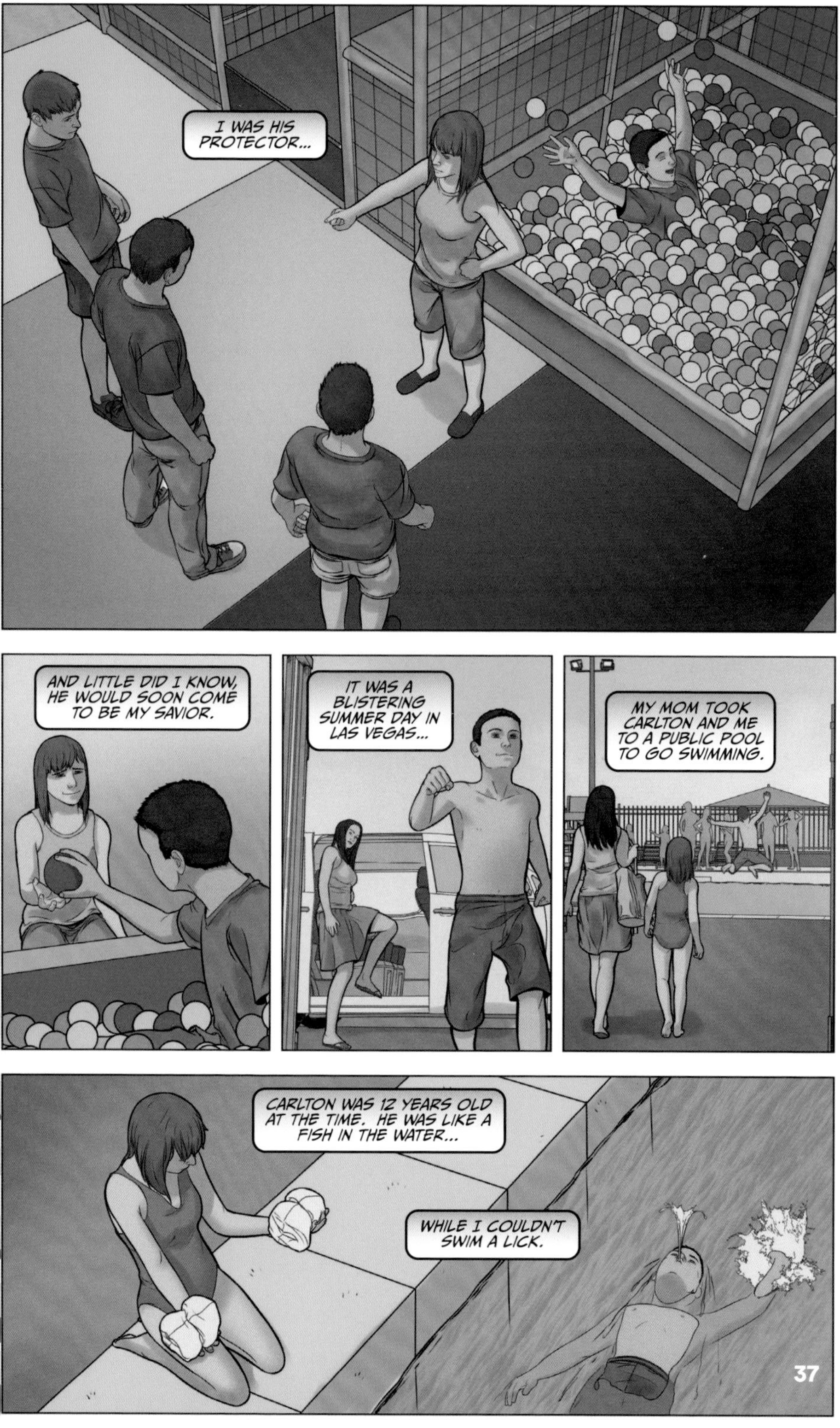
I WAS HIS PROTECTOR...
AND LITTLE DID I KNOW, HE WOULD SOON COME TO BE MY SAVIOR.
IT WAS A BLISTERING SUMMER DAY IN LAS VEGAS...
MY MOM TOOK CARLTON AND ME TO A PUBLIC POOL TO GO SWIMMING.
CARLTON WAS 12 YEARS OLD AT THE TIME. HE WAS LIKE A FISH IN THE WATER...
WHILE I COULDN'T SWIM A LICK.

TURNS OUT, I COULDN'T WEAR MY FLOATIES THAT AFTERNOON...

THE POSTED SIGN SAID THEY WERE "TOO DANGEROUS."

MY BROTHER AND I WERE HAVING FUN PLAYING A GAME IN THE POOL.

AS WE WERE PLAYING, I FOUND MYSELF DRIFTING INTO THE DEEP END...

I STARTED TO PANIC A LITTLE.

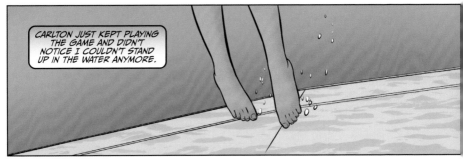

CARLTON JUST KEPT PLAYING THE GAME AND DIDN'T NOTICE I COULDN'T STAND UP IN THE WATER ANYMORE.

WHEN HE LOOKED OVER TO ME, HE COULD SEE ME AS I BEGAN TO SPLASH AROUND TRYING TO KEEP AFLOAT...

AT FIRST IT SEEMED LIKE HE WASN'T SURE IF I WAS STILL PLAYING OR IF I WAS SERIOUS.

THEN CARLTON STARTED TO FLAP IN THE WATER WITH CONCERN.

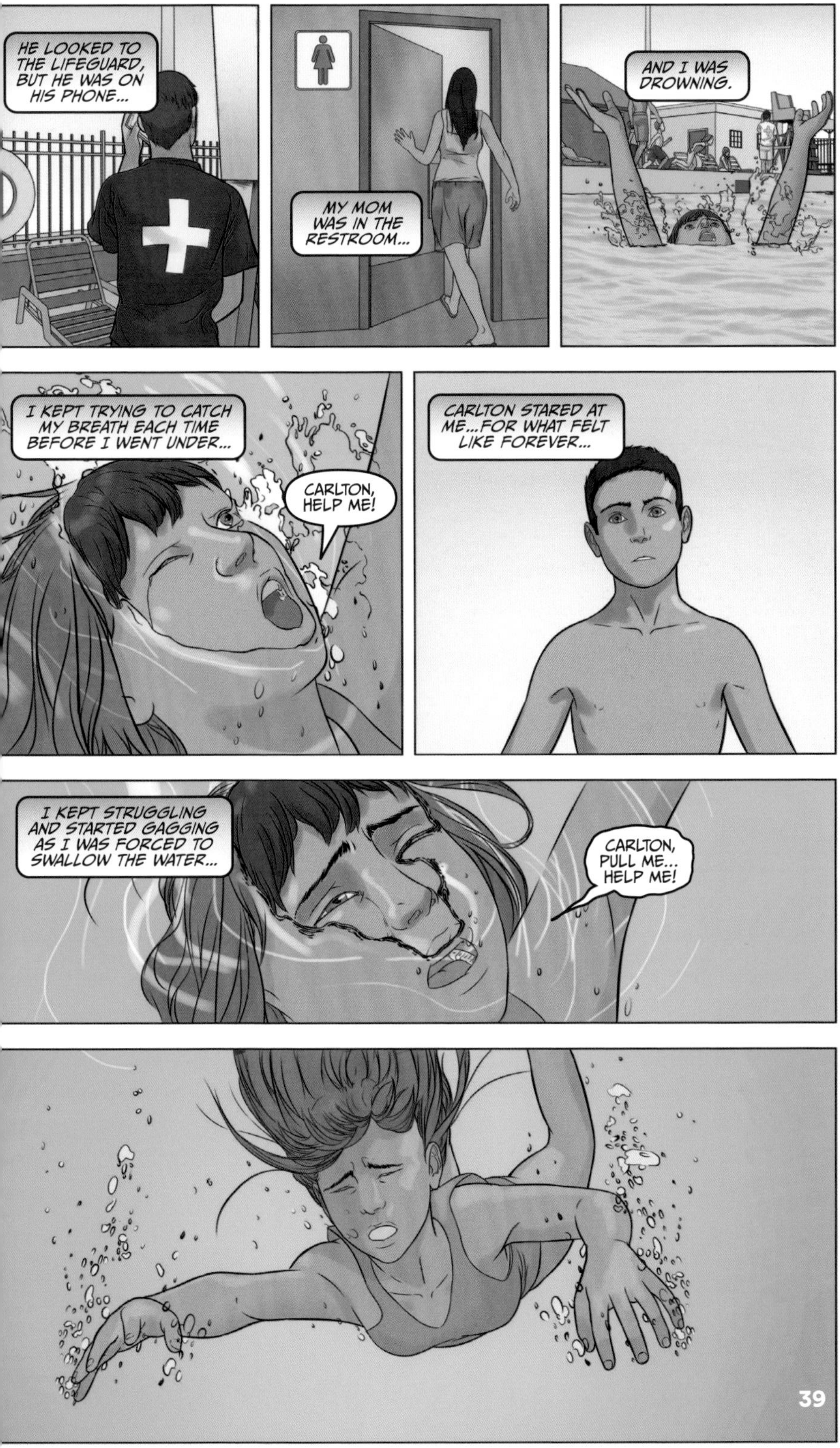
HE LOOKED TO THE LIFEGUARD, BUT HE WAS ON HIS PHONE...
MY MOM WAS IN THE RESTROOM...
AND I WAS DROWNING.
I KEPT TRYING TO CATCH MY BREATH EACH TIME BEFORE I WENT UNDER...
CARLTON, HELP ME!
CARLTON STARED AT ME...FOR WHAT FELT LIKE FOREVER...
I KEPT STRUGGLING AND STARTED GAGGING AS I WAS FORCED TO SWALLOW THE WATER...
CARLTON, PULL ME... HELP ME!

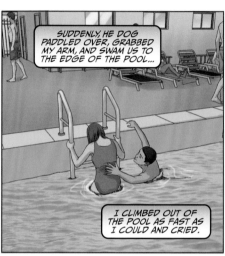

SUDDENLY, HE DOG PADDLED OVER, GRABBED MY ARM, AND SWAM US TO THE EDGE OF THE POOL...

I CLIMBED OUT OF THE POOL AS FAST AS I COULD AND CRIED.

CARLTON SAT DOWN NEXT TO ME...

...HEAD DOWN... ROCKING IN SHOCK.

NOT ONLY DID CARLTON SAVE ME...HE UNDERSTOOD I WAS IN TROUBLE AND ACTED...

....JUST LIKE A NORMAL TWELVE-YEAR-OLD.

SUDDENLY, "DIFFERENT," "SPECIAL," OR "A CHILD WITH AUTISM" WERE JUST LABELS...

AUTISM

DIFFERENT

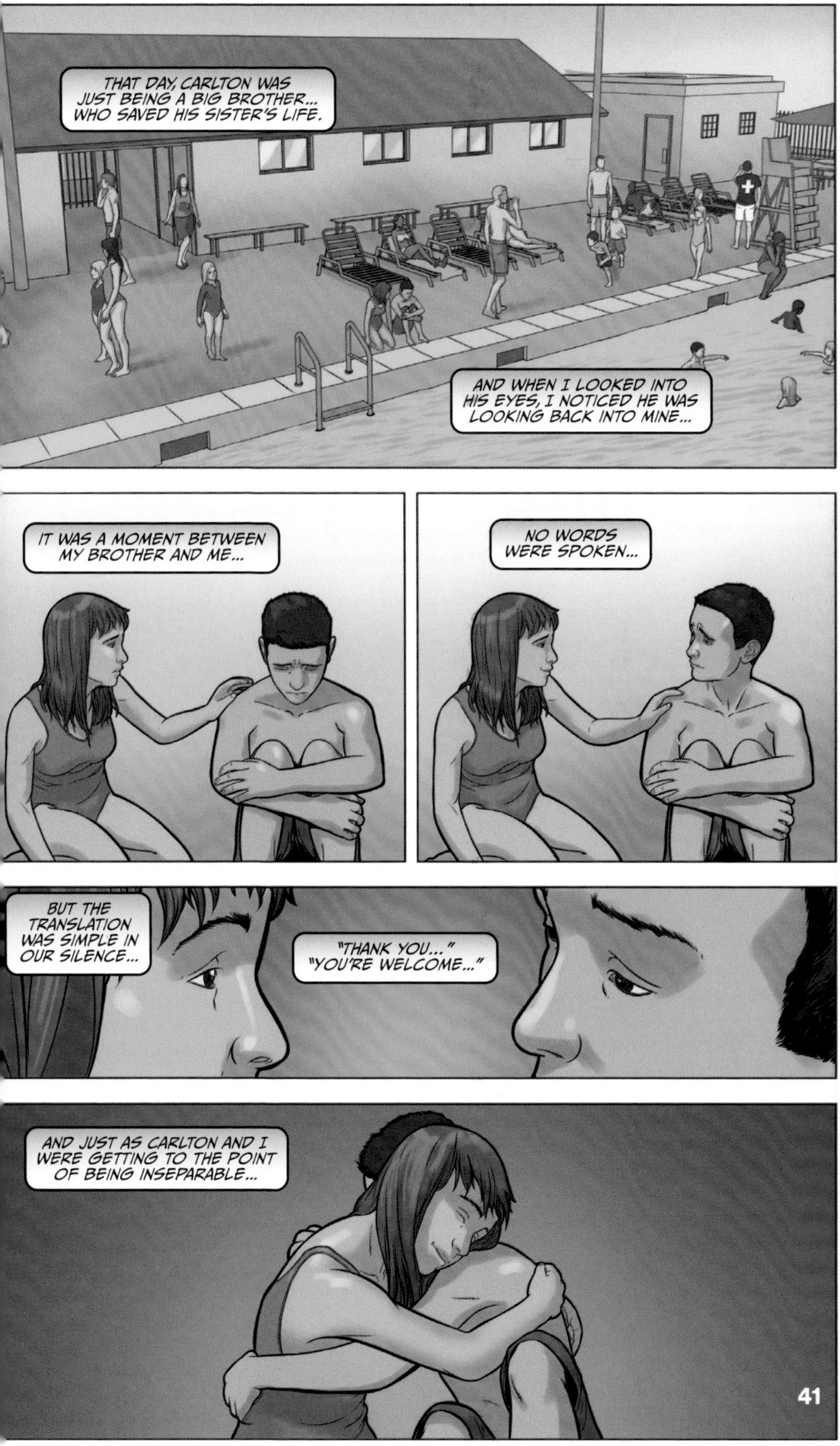
THAT DAY, CARLTON WAS JUST BEING A BIG BROTHER... WHO SAVED HIS SISTER'S LIFE.
AND WHEN I LOOKED INTO HIS EYES, I NOTICED HE WAS LOOKING BACK INTO MINE...
IT WAS A MOMENT BETWEEN MY BROTHER AND ME...
NO WORDS WERE SPOKEN...
BUT THE TRANSLATION WAS SIMPLE IN OUR SILENCE...
"THANK YOU..." "YOU'RE WELCOME..."
AND JUST AS CARLTON AND I WERE GETTING TO THE POINT OF BEING INSEPARABLE...

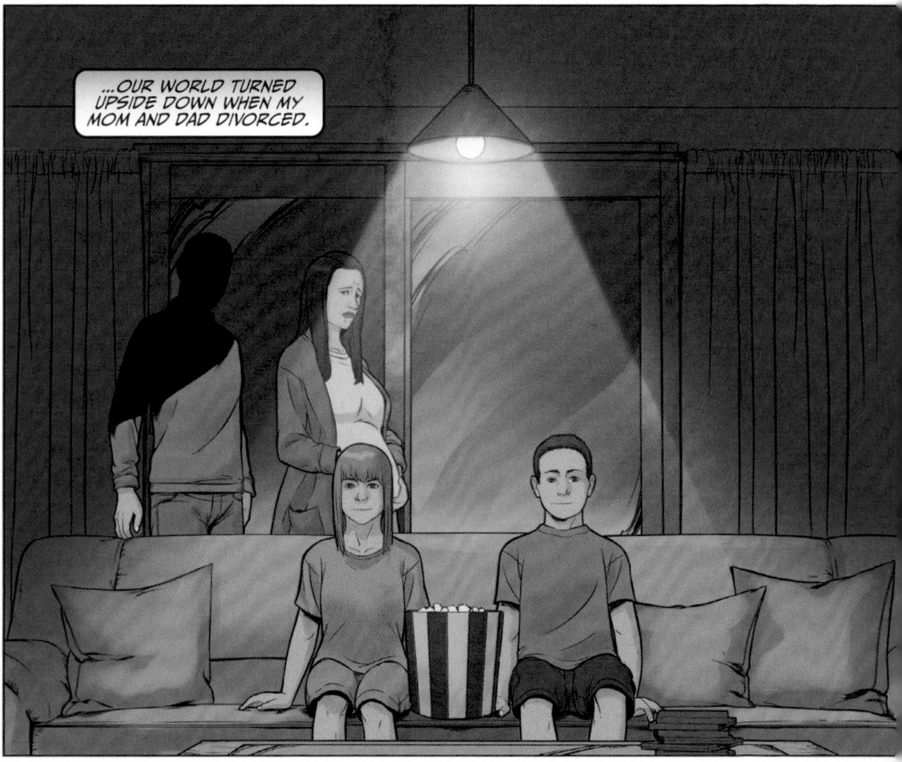
...OUR WORLD TURNED UPSIDE DOWN WHEN MY MOM AND DAD DIVORCED.

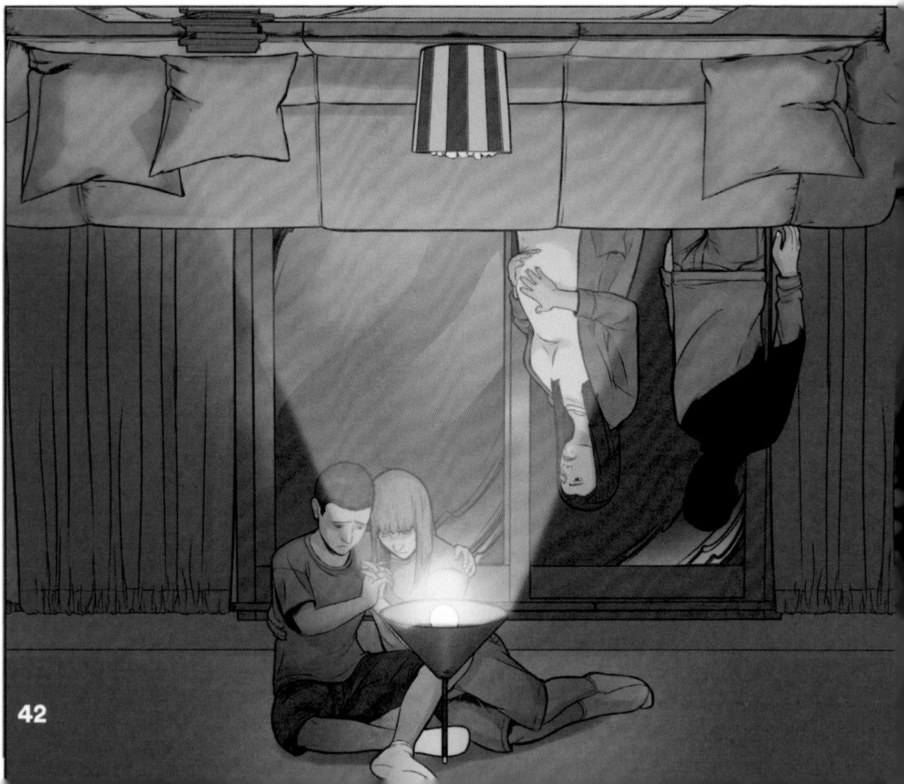

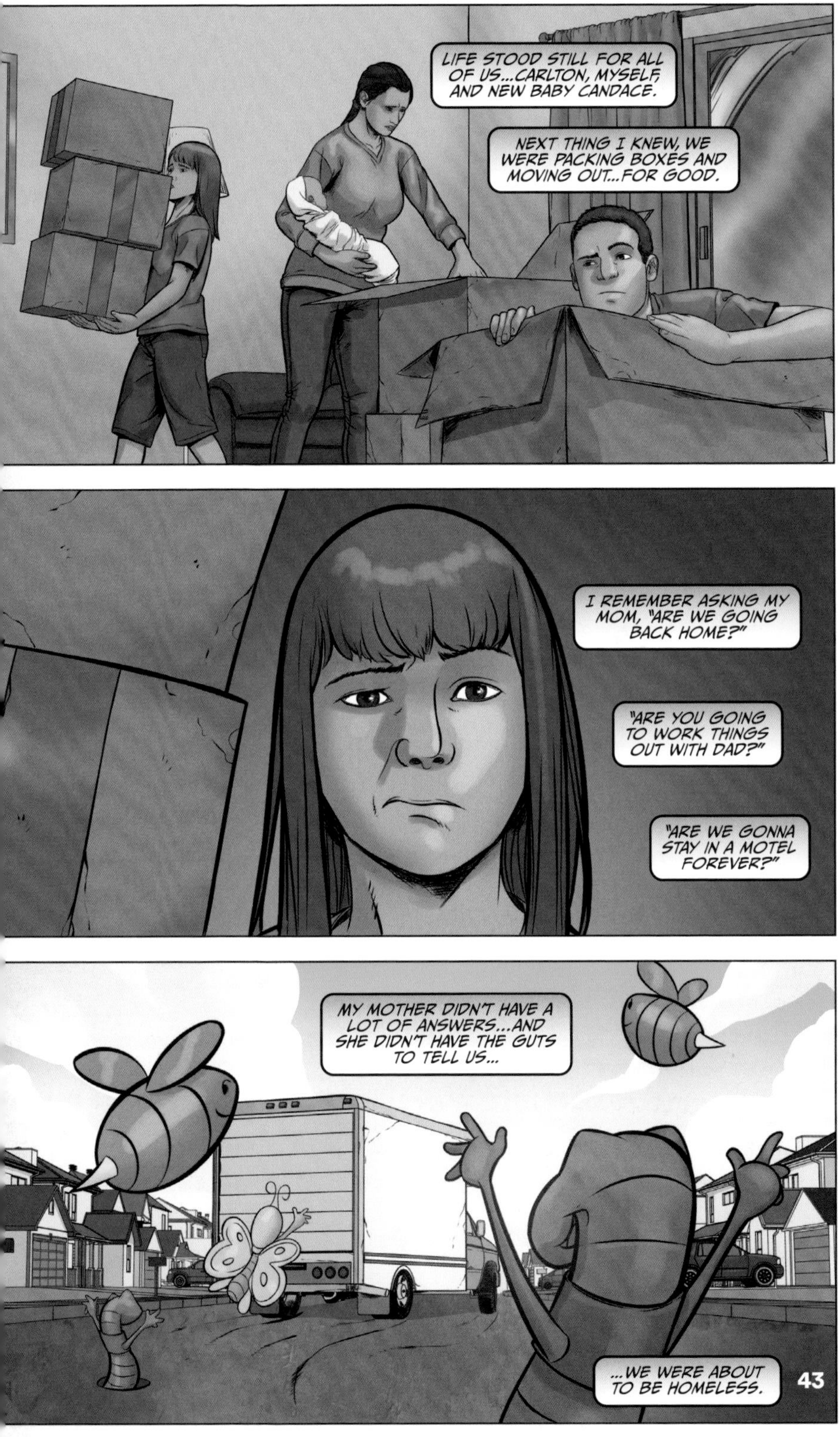
LIFE STOOD STILL FOR ALL OF US...CARLTON, MYSELF, AND NEW BABY CANDACE.
NEXT THING I KNEW, WE WERE PACKING BOXES AND MOVING OUT...FOR GOOD.
I REMEMBER ASKING MY MOM, "ARE WE GOING BACK HOME?"
"ARE YOU GOING TO WORK THINGS OUT WITH DAD?"
"ARE WE GONNA STAY IN A MOTEL FOREVER?"
MY MOTHER DIDN'T HAVE A LOT OF ANSWERS...AND SHE DIDN'T HAVE THE GUTS TO TELL US...
...WE WERE ABOUT TO BE HOMELESS.

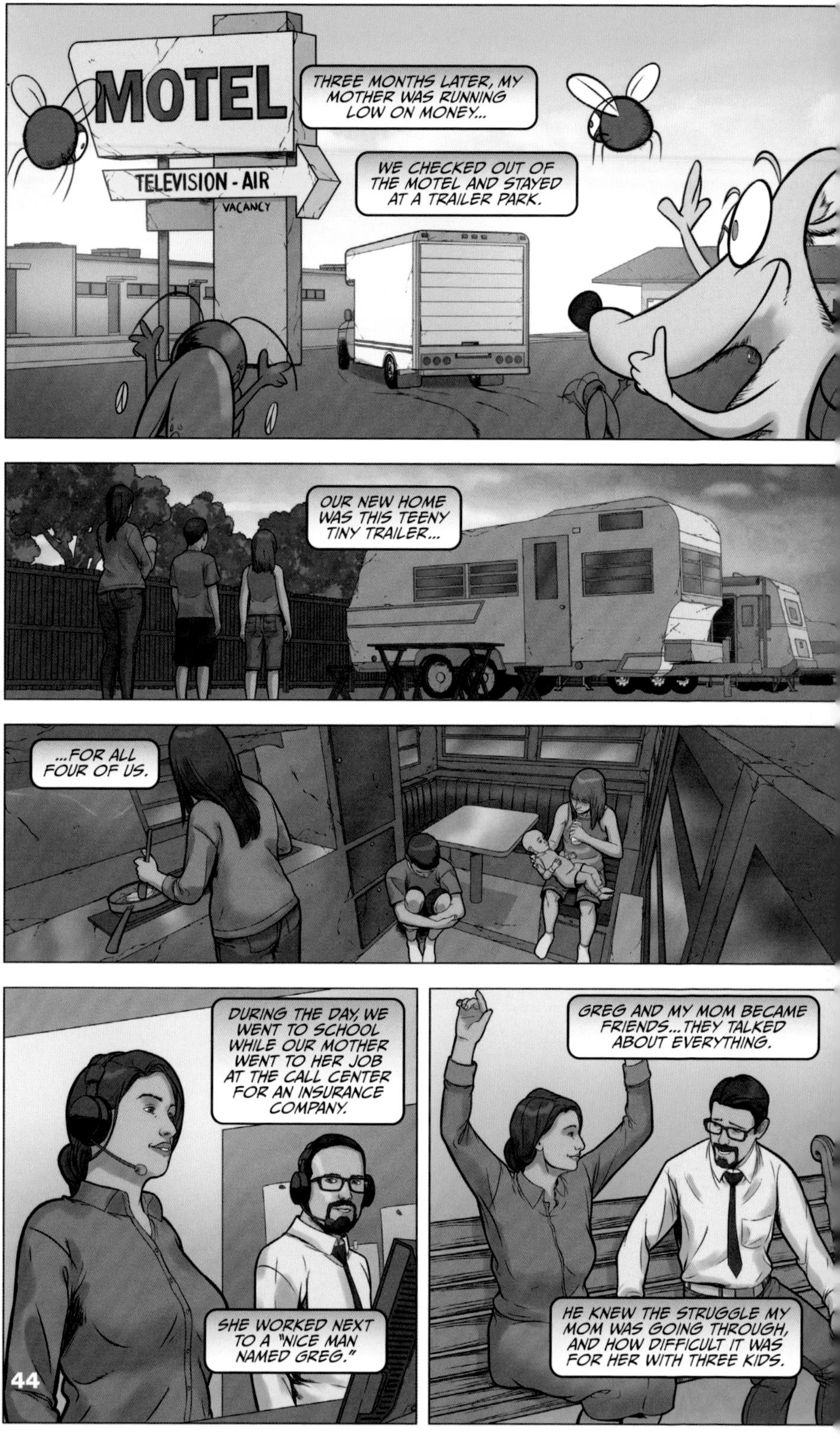
MOTEL
TELEVISION - AIR
VACANCY
THREE MONTHS LATER, MY MOTHER WAS RUNNING LOW ON MONEY...
WE CHECKED OUT OF THE MOTEL AND STAYED AT A TRAILER PARK.
OUR NEW HOME WAS THIS TEENY TINY TRAILER...
...FOR ALL FOUR OF US.
DURING THE DAY, WE WENT TO SCHOOL WHILE OUR MOTHER WENT TO HER JOB AT THE CALL CENTER FOR AN INSURANCE COMPANY.
SHE WORKED NEXT TO A "NICE MAN NAMED GREG."
GREG AND MY MOM BECAME FRIENDS...THEY TALKED ABOUT EVERYTHING.
HE KNEW THE STRUGGLE MY MOM WAS GOING THROUGH, AND HOW DIFFICULT IT WAS FOR HER WITH THREE KIDS.

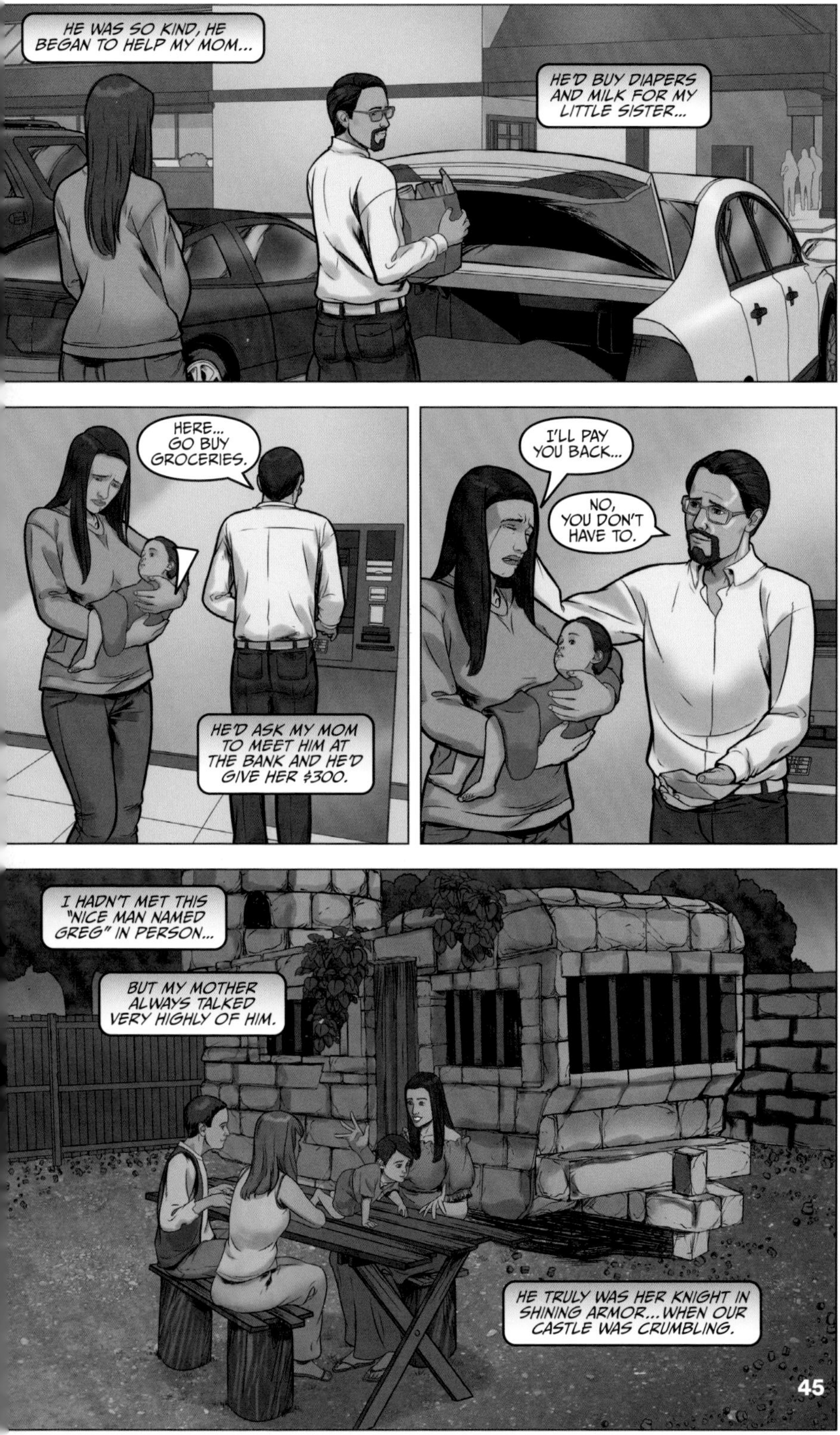
HE WAS SO KIND, HE BEGAN TO HELP MY MOM...
HE'D BUY DIAPERS AND MILK FOR MY LITTLE SISTER...
HERE... GO BUY GROCERIES.
HE'D ASK MY MOM TO MEET HIM AT THE BANK AND HE'D GIVE HER $300.
I'LL PAY YOU BACK...
NO, YOU DON'T HAVE TO.
I HADN'T MET THIS "NICE MAN NAMED GREG" IN PERSON...
BUT MY MOTHER ALWAYS TALKED VERY HIGHLY OF HIM.
HE TRULY WAS HER KNIGHT IN SHINING ARMOR...WHEN OUR CASTLE WAS CRUMBLING.

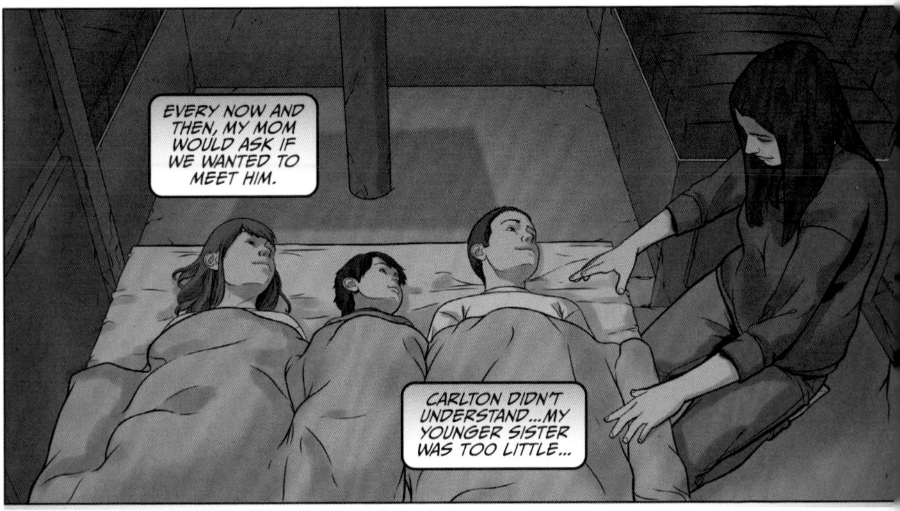
EVERY NOW AND THEN, MY MOM WOULD ASK IF WE WANTED TO MEET HIM.
CARLTON DIDN'T UNDERSTAND...MY YOUNGER SISTER WAS TOO LITTLE...

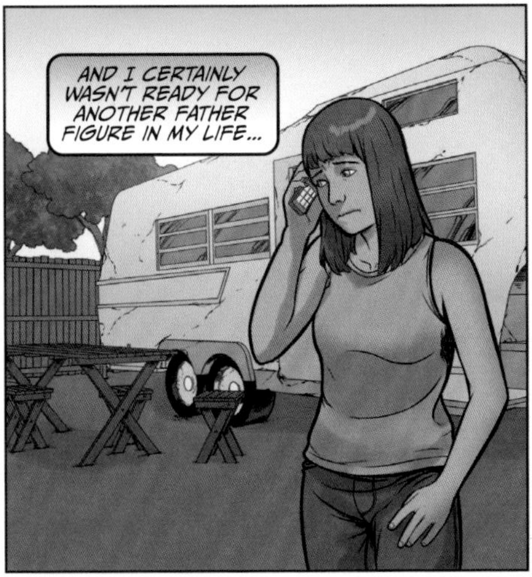
AND I CERTAINLY WASN'T READY FOR ANOTHER FATHER FIGURE IN MY LIFE...

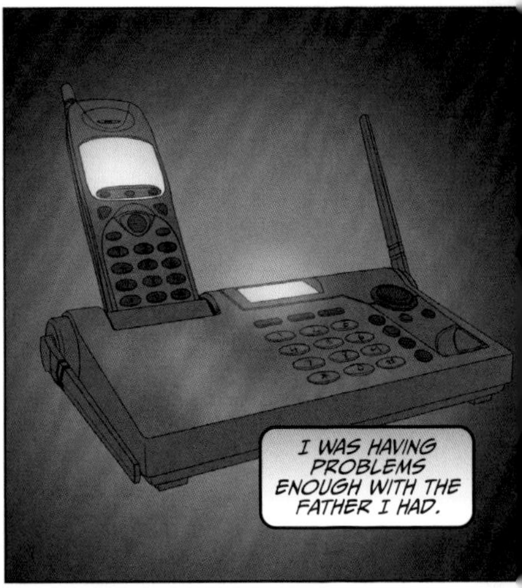
I WAS HAVING PROBLEMS ENOUGH WITH THE FATHER I HAD.

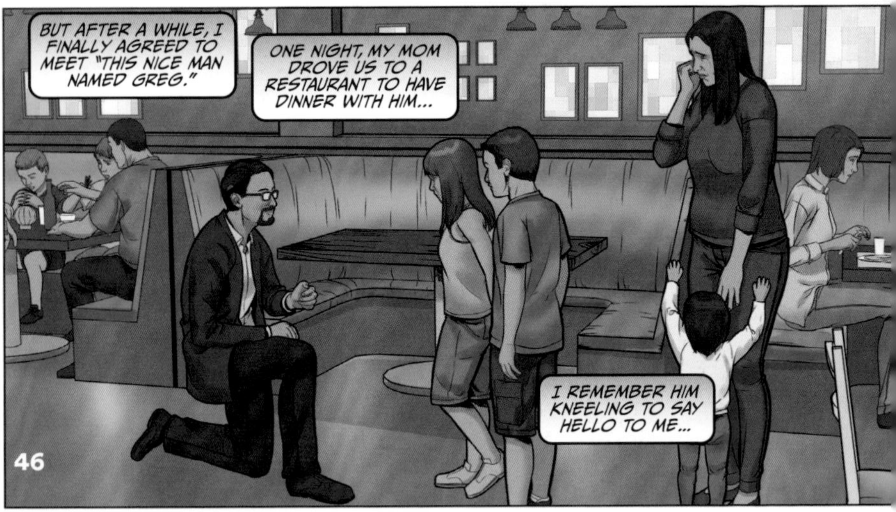
BUT AFTER A WHILE, I FINALLY AGREED TO MEET "THIS NICE MAN NAMED GREG."
ONE NIGHT, MY MOM DROVE US TO A RESTAURANT TO HAVE DINNER WITH HIM...
I REMEMBER HIM KNEELING TO SAY HELLO TO ME...

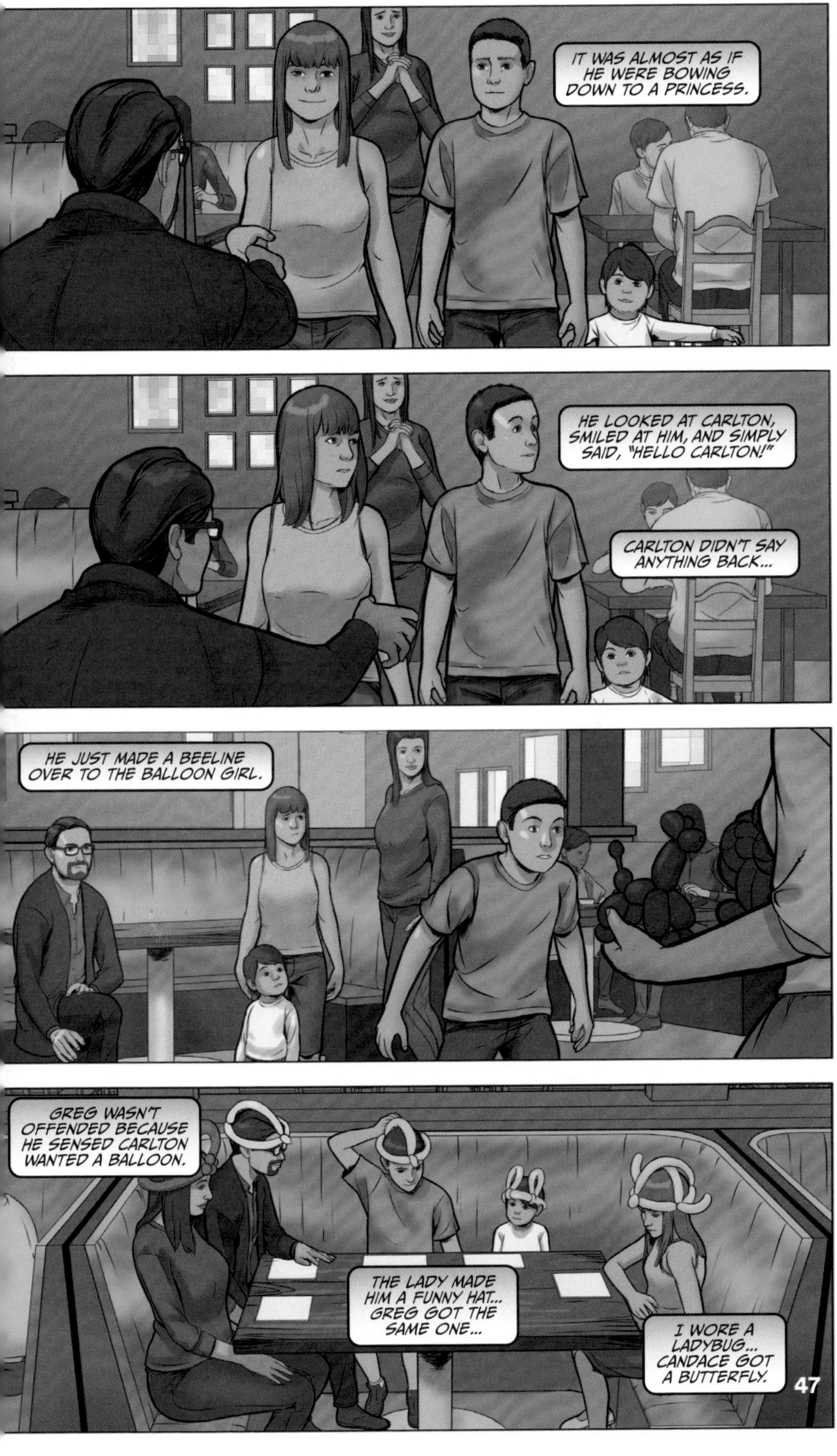
IT WAS ALMOST AS IF HE WERE BOWING DOWN TO A PRINCESS.
HE LOOKED AT CARLTON, SMILED AT HIM, AND SIMPLY SAID, "HELLO CARLTON!"
CARLTON DIDN'T SAY ANYTHING BACK...
HE JUST MADE A BEELINE OVER TO THE BALLOON GIRL.
GREG WASN'T OFFENDED BECAUSE HE SENSED CARLTON WANTED A BALLOON.
THE LADY MADE HIM A FUNNY HAT... GREG GOT THE SAME ONE...
I WORE A LADYBUG... CANDACE GOT A BUTTERFLY.

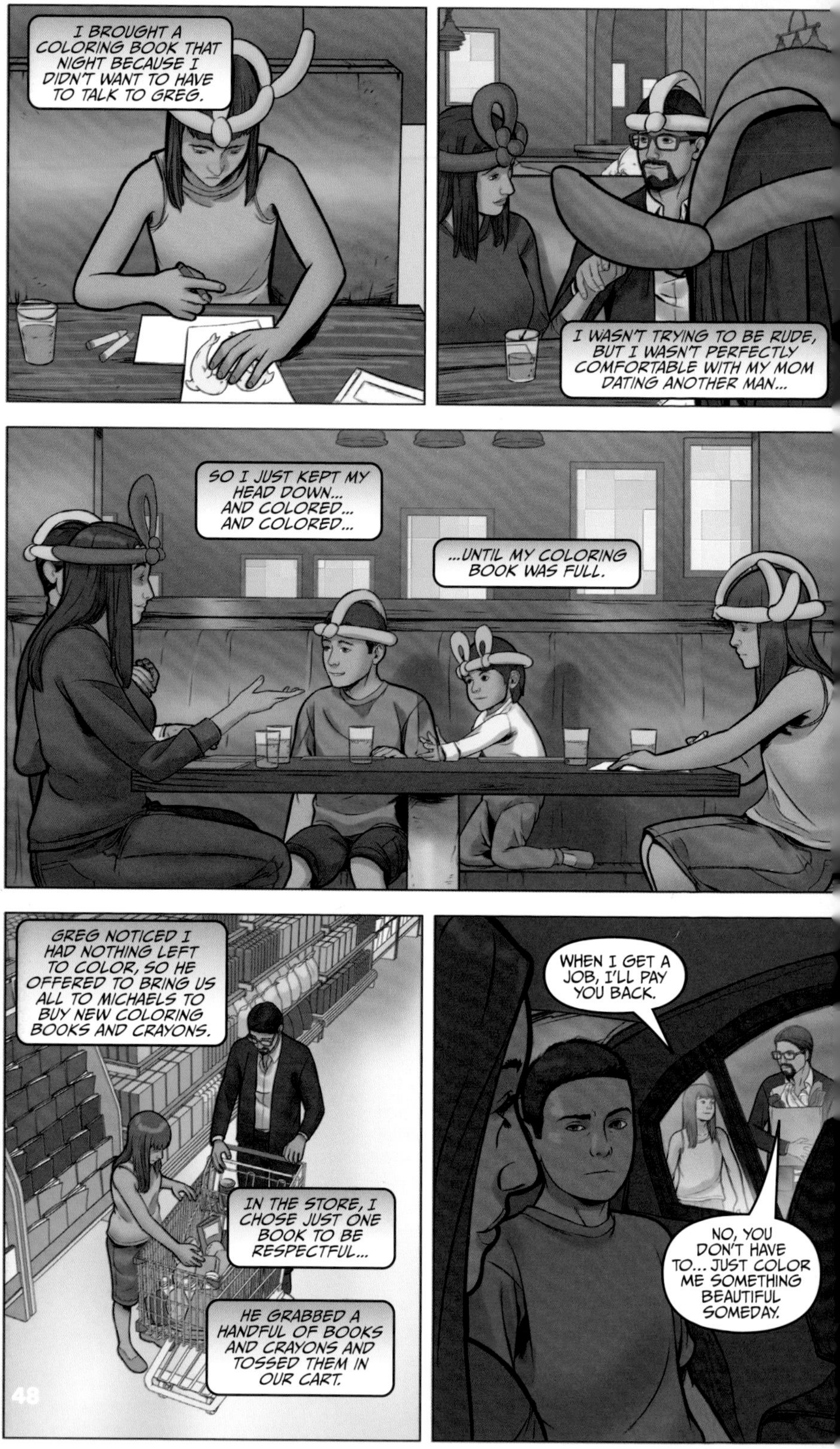
I BROUGHT A COLORING BOOK THAT NIGHT BECAUSE I DIDN'T WANT TO HAVE TO TALK TO GREG.
I WASN'T TRYING TO BE RUDE, BUT I WASN'T PERFECTLY COMFORTABLE WITH MY MOM DATING ANOTHER MAN...
SO I JUST KEPT MY HEAD DOWN... AND COLORED... AND COLORED...
...UNTIL MY COLORING BOOK WAS FULL.
GREG NOTICED I HAD NOTHING LEFT TO COLOR, SO HE OFFERED TO BRING US ALL TO MICHAELS TO BUY NEW COLORING BOOKS AND CRAYONS.
IN THE STORE, I CHOSE JUST ONE BOOK TO BE RESPECTFUL...
HE GRABBED A HANDFUL OF BOOKS AND CRAYONS AND TOSSED THEM IN OUR CART.
WHEN I GET A JOB, I'LL PAY YOU BACK.
NO, YOU DON'T HAVE TO... JUST COLOR ME SOMETHING BEAUTIFUL SOMEDAY.

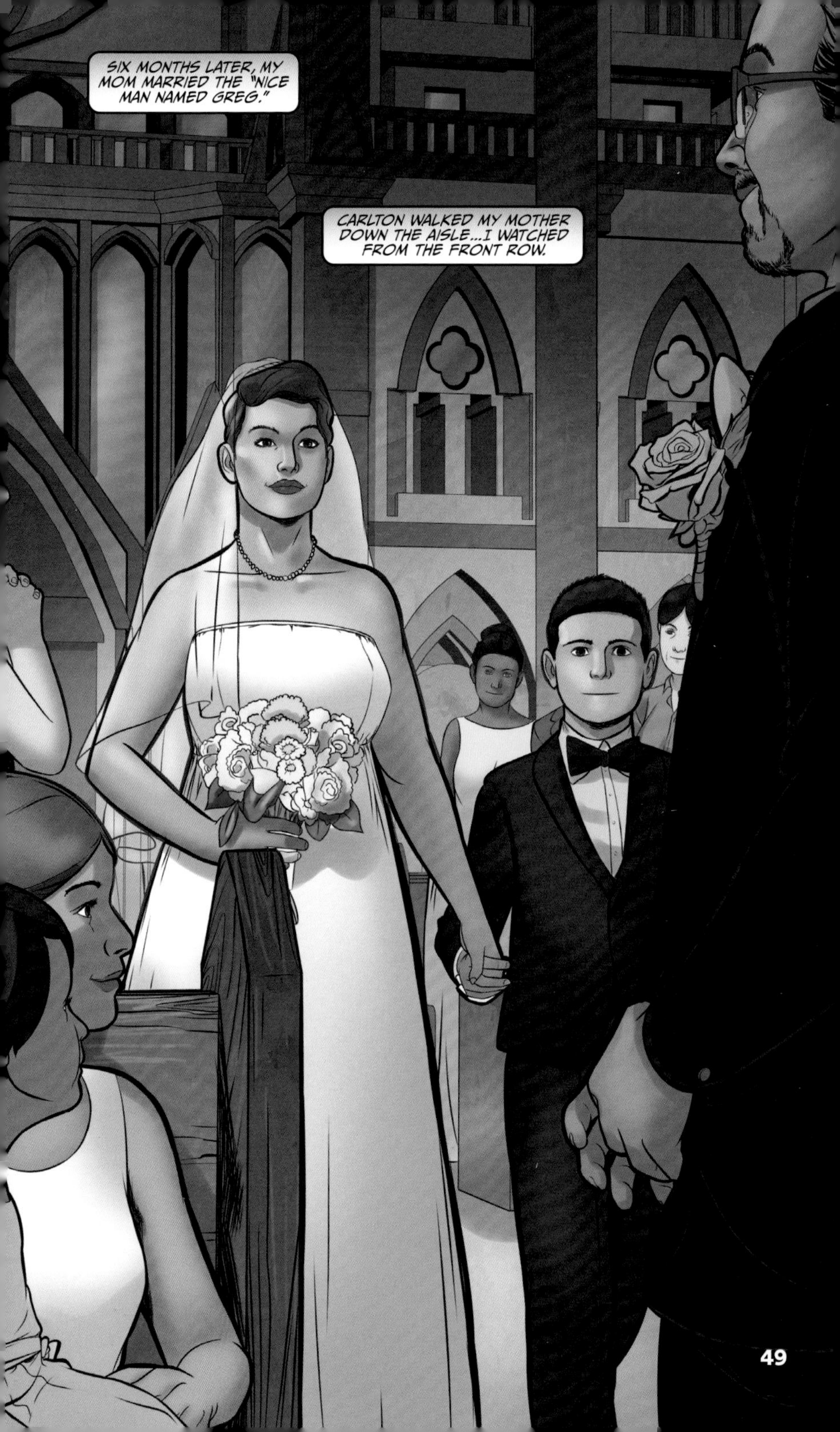
SIX MONTHS LATER, MY MOM MARRIED THE "NICE MAN NAMED GREG."
CARLTON WALKED MY MOTHER DOWN THE AISLE...I WATCHED FROM THE FRONT ROW.

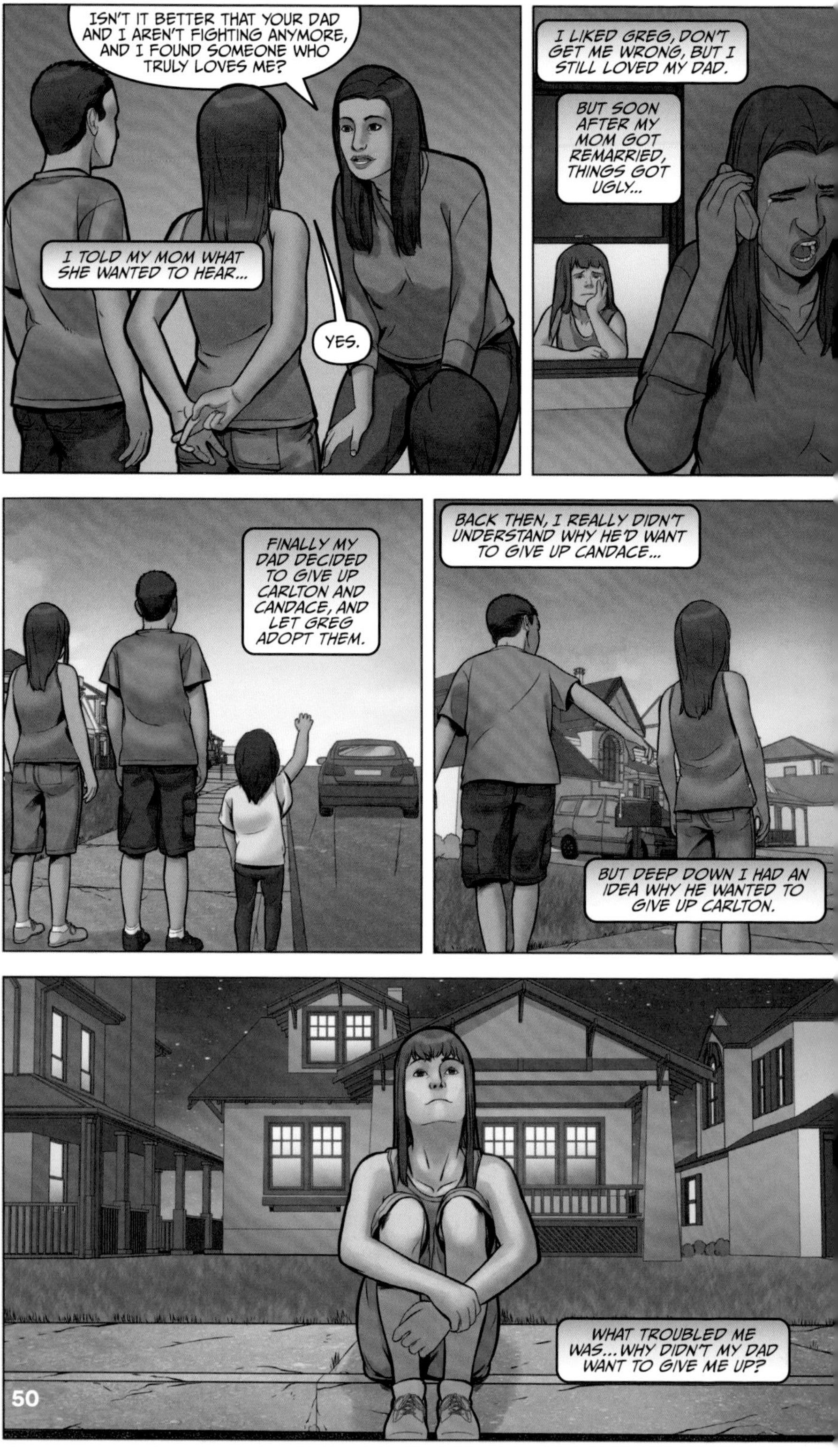
ISN'T IT BETTER THAT YOUR DAD AND I AREN'T FIGHTING ANYMORE, AND I FOUND SOMEONE WHO TRULY LOVES ME?
I TOLD MY MOM WHAT SHE WANTED TO HEAR...
YES.
I LIKED GREG, DON'T GET ME WRONG, BUT I STILL LOVED MY DAD.
BUT SOON AFTER MY MOM GOT REMARRIED, THINGS GOT UGLY...
FINALLY MY DAD DECIDED TO GIVE UP CARLTON AND CANDACE, AND LET GREG ADOPT THEM.
BACK THEN, I REALLY DIDN'T UNDERSTAND WHY HE'D WANT TO GIVE UP CANDACE...
BUT DEEP DOWN I HAD AN IDEA WHY HE WANTED TO GIVE UP CARLTON.
WHAT TROUBLED ME WAS...WHY DIDN'T MY DAD WANT TO GIVE ME UP?

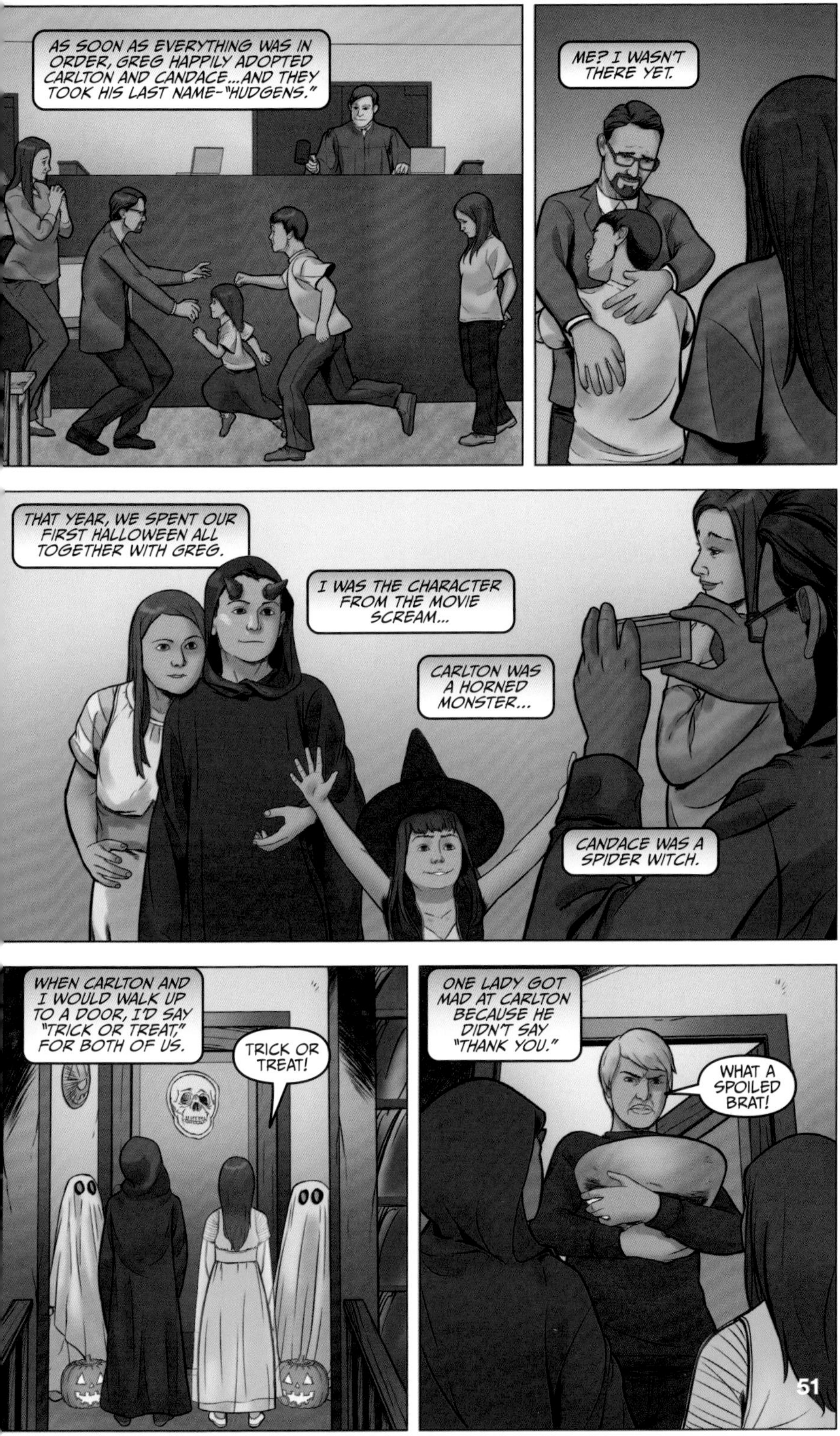
AS SOON AS EVERYTHING WAS IN ORDER, GREG HAPPILY ADOPTED CARLTON AND CANDACE...AND THEY TOOK HIS LAST NAME–"HUDGENS."
ME? I WASN'T THERE YET.
THAT YEAR, WE SPENT OUR FIRST HALLOWEEN ALL TOGETHER WITH GREG.
I WAS THE CHARACTER FROM THE MOVIE SCREAM...
CARLTON WAS A HORNED MONSTER...
CANDACE WAS A SPIDER WITCH.
WHEN CARLTON AND I WOULD WALK UP TO A DOOR, I'D SAY "TRICK OR TREAT," FOR BOTH OF US.
TRICK OR TREAT!
ONE LADY GOT MAD AT CARLTON BECAUSE HE DIDN'T SAY "THANK YOU."
WHAT A SPOILED BRAT!

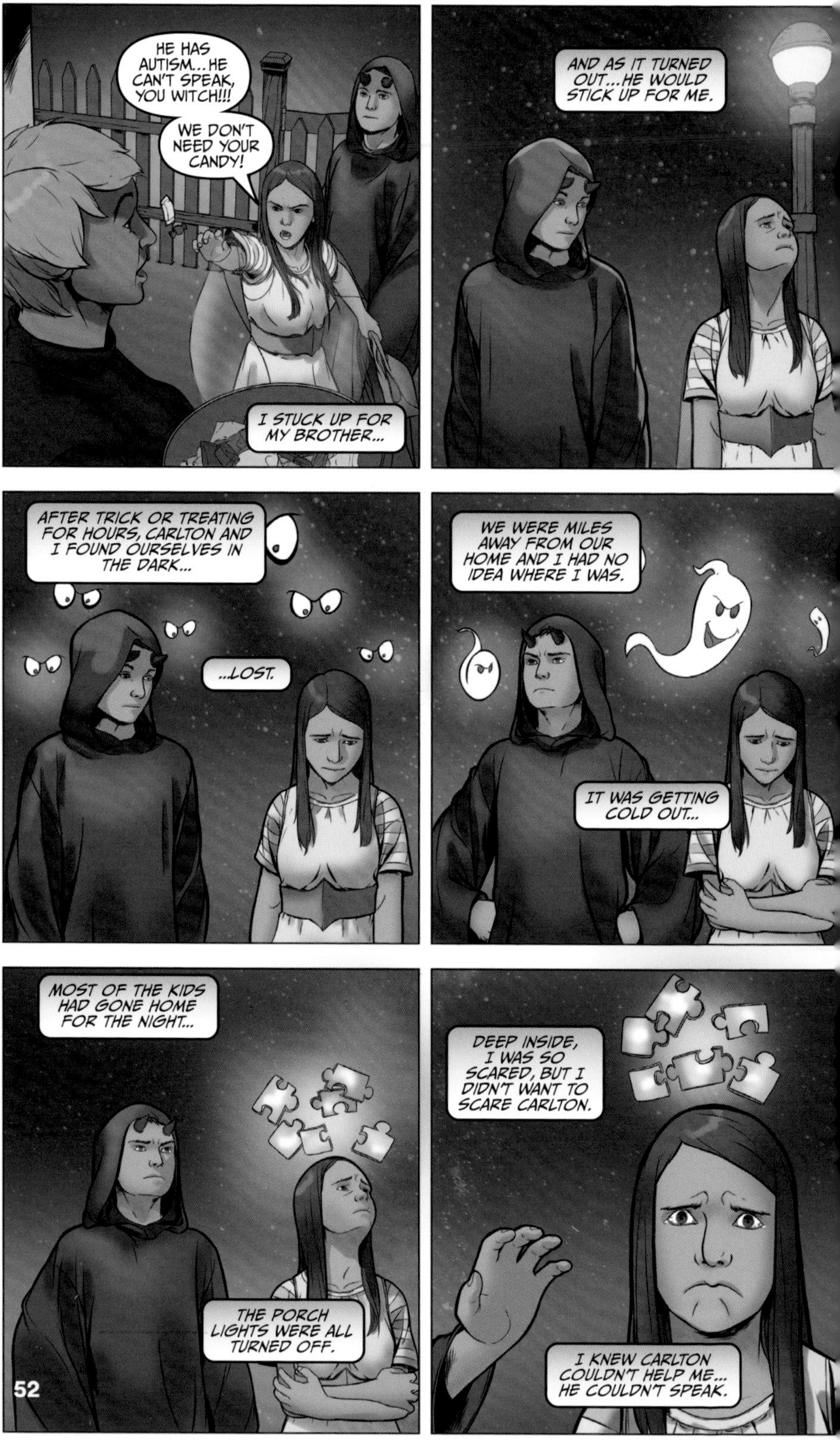
HE HAS AUTISM...HE CAN'T SPEAK, YOU WITCH!!!
WE DON'T NEED YOUR CANDY!
I STUCK UP FOR MY BROTHER...
AND AS IT TURNED OUT...HE WOULD STICK UP FOR ME.
AFTER TRICK OR TREATING FOR HOURS, CARLTON AND I FOUND OURSELVES IN THE DARK...
...LOST.
WE WERE MILES AWAY FROM OUR HOME AND I HAD NO IDEA WHERE I WAS.
IT WAS GETTING COLD OUT...
MOST OF THE KIDS HAD GONE HOME FOR THE NIGHT...
THE PORCH LIGHTS WERE ALL TURNED OFF.
DEEP INSIDE, I WAS SO SCARED, BUT I DIDN'T WANT TO SCARE CARLTON.
I KNEW CARLTON COULDN'T HELP ME... HE COULDN'T SPEAK.

BUT, HE DIDN'T HAVE TO...

HE COULD SENSE I WAS UNSURE OF WHERE WE WERE AS I LOOKED AROUND NOT KNOWING WHICH WAY TO GO.

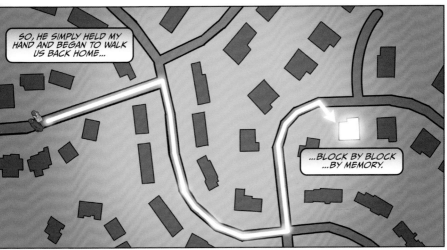

SO, HE SIMPLY HELD MY HAND AND BEGAN TO WALK US BACK HOME...

...BLOCK BY BLOCK ...BY MEMORY.

AND WHEN I SAW OUR HOUSE, I THOUGHT TO MYSELF...

...CARLTON TRULY IS MY GUARDIAN ANGEL...

...AN ANGEL SENT DOWN FROM THE HEAVENS...

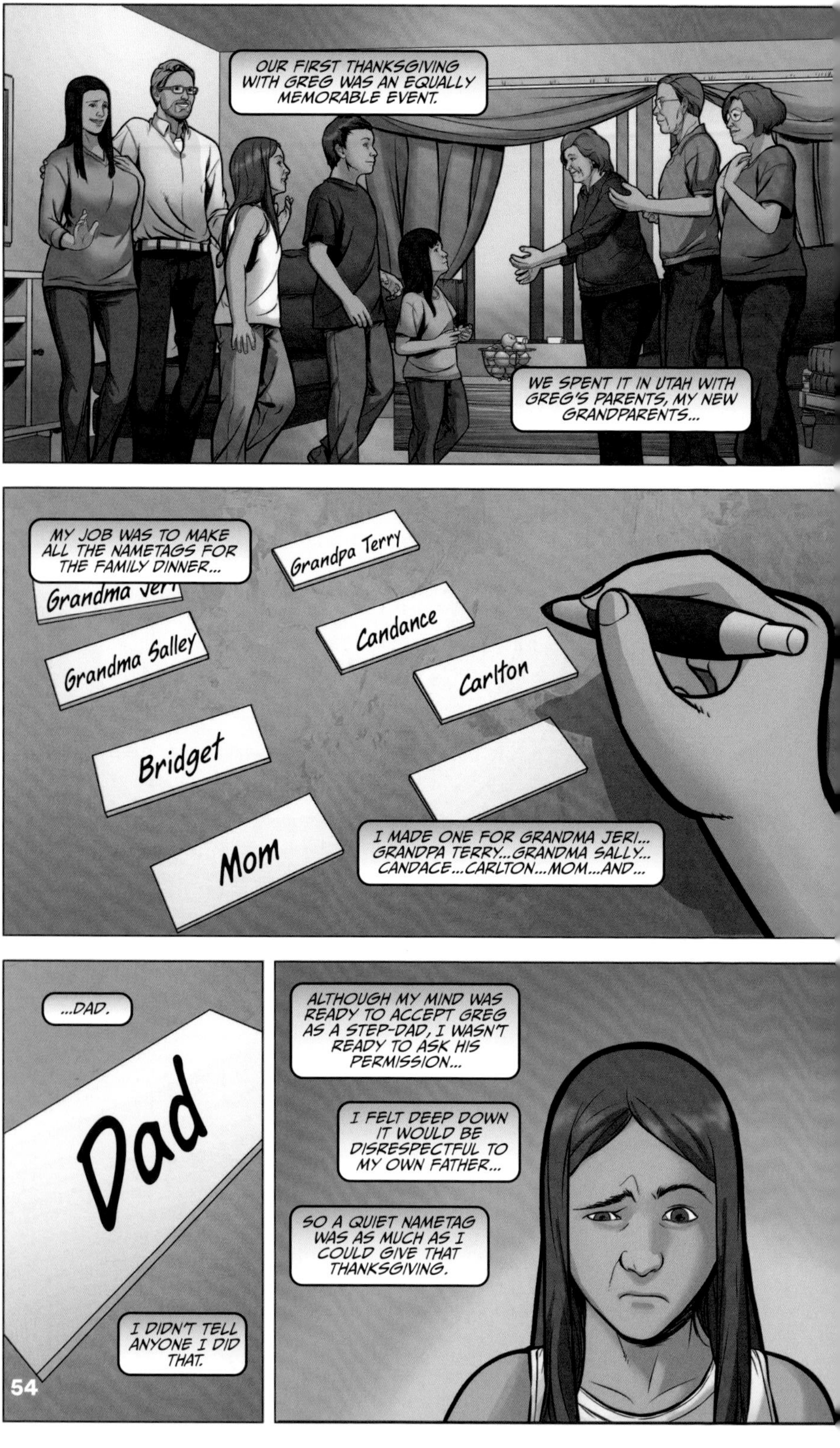
OUR FIRST THANKSGIVING WITH GREG WAS AN EQUALLY MEMORABLE EVENT.
WE SPENT IT IN UTAH WITH GREG'S PARENTS, MY NEW GRANDPARENTS...
MY JOB WAS TO MAKE ALL THE NAMETAGS FOR THE FAMILY DINNER...
Grandpa Terry
Grandma Jer
Candance
Grandma Salley
Carlton
Bridget
Mom
I MADE ONE FOR GRANDMA JERI... GRANDPA TERRY...GRANDMA SALLY... CANDACE...CARLTON...MOM...AND...
...DAD.
Dad
I DIDN'T TELL ANYONE I DID THAT.
ALTHOUGH MY MIND WAS READY TO ACCEPT GREG AS A STEP-DAD, I WASN'T READY TO ASK HIS PERMISSION...
I FELT DEEP DOWN IT WOULD BE DISRESPECTFUL TO MY OWN FATHER...
SO A QUIET NAMETAG WAS AS MUCH AS I COULD GIVE THAT THANKSGIVING.

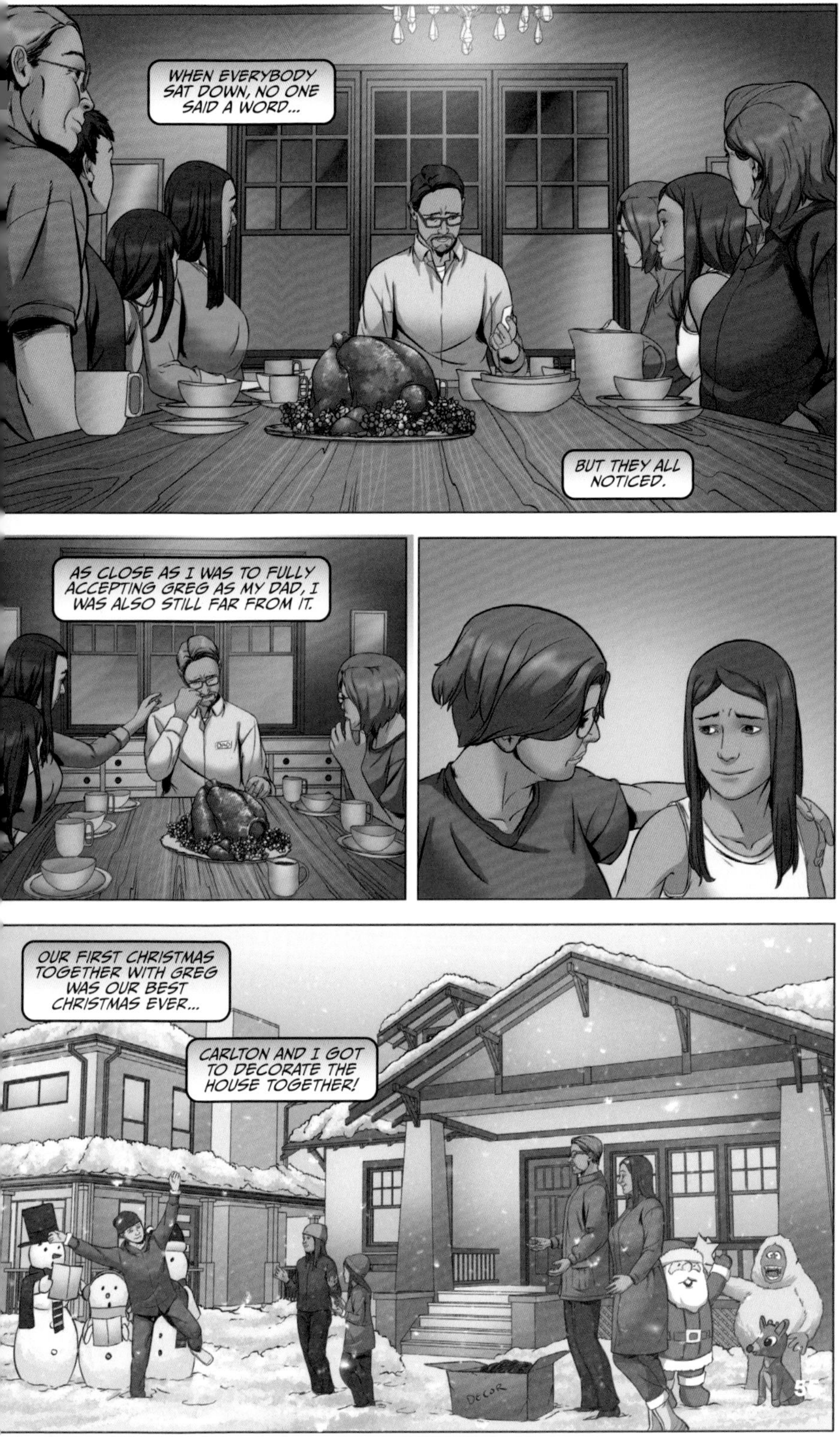
WHEN EVERYBODY SAT DOWN, NO ONE SAID A WORD...
BUT THEY ALL NOTICED.
AS CLOSE AS I WAS TO FULLY ACCEPTING GREG AS MY DAD, I WAS ALSO STILL FAR FROM IT.
OUR FIRST CHRISTMAS TOGETHER WITH GREG WAS OUR BEST CHRISTMAS EVER...
CARLTON AND I GOT TO DECORATE THE HOUSE TOGETHER!
DECOR

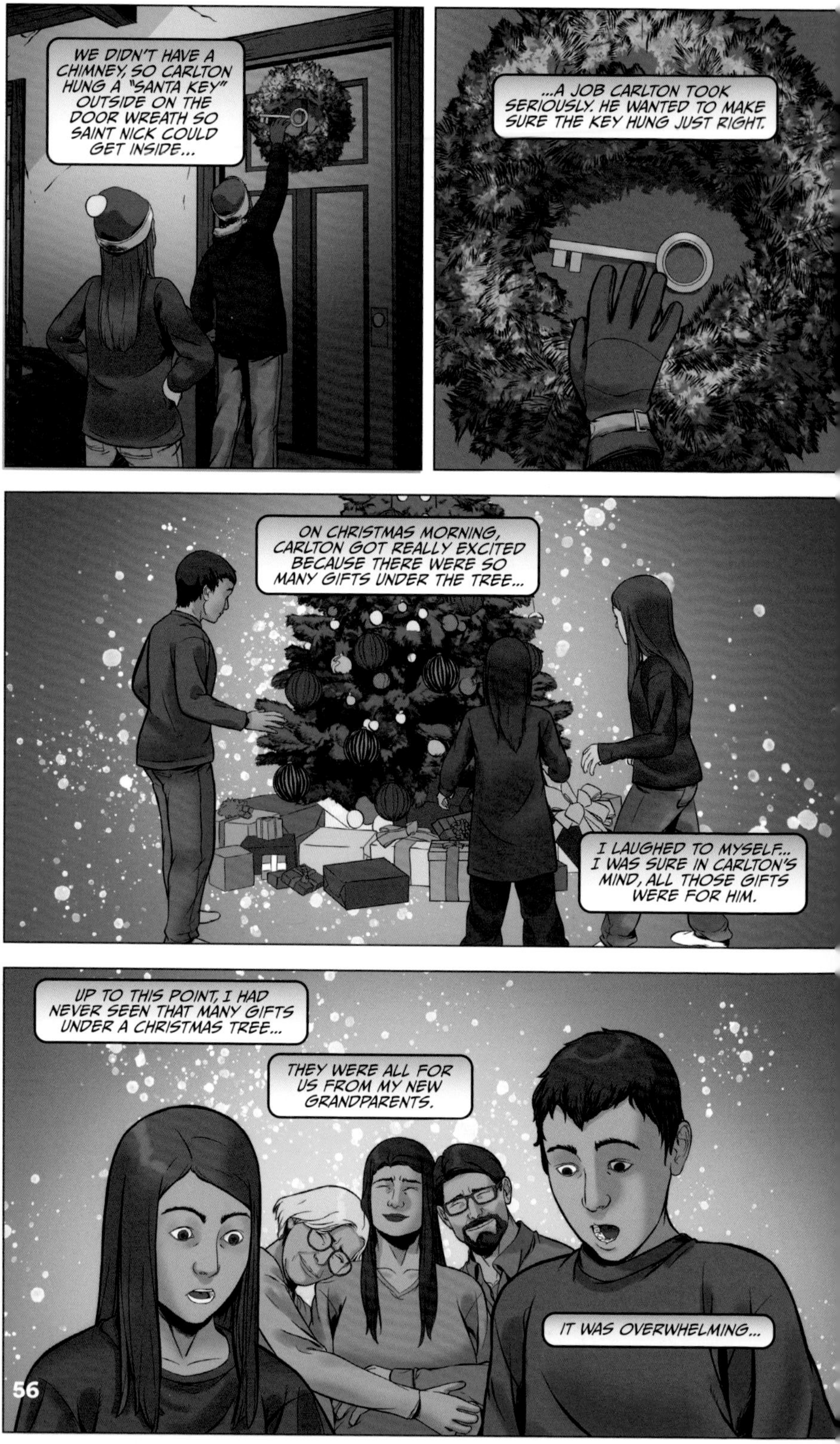
WE DIDN'T HAVE A CHIMNEY, SO CARLTON HUNG A "SANTA KEY" OUTSIDE ON THE DOOR WREATH SO SAINT NICK COULD GET INSIDE...
...A JOB CARLTON TOOK SERIOUSLY. HE WANTED TO MAKE SURE THE KEY HUNG JUST RIGHT.
ON CHRISTMAS MORNING, CARLTON GOT REALLY EXCITED BECAUSE THERE WERE SO MANY GIFTS UNDER THE TREE...
I LAUGHED TO MYSELF... I WAS SURE IN CARLTON'S MIND, ALL THOSE GIFTS WERE FOR HIM.
UP TO THIS POINT, I HAD NEVER SEEN THAT MANY GIFTS UNDER A CHRISTMAS TREE...
THEY WERE ALL FOR US FROM MY NEW GRANDPARENTS.
IT WAS OVERWHELMING...

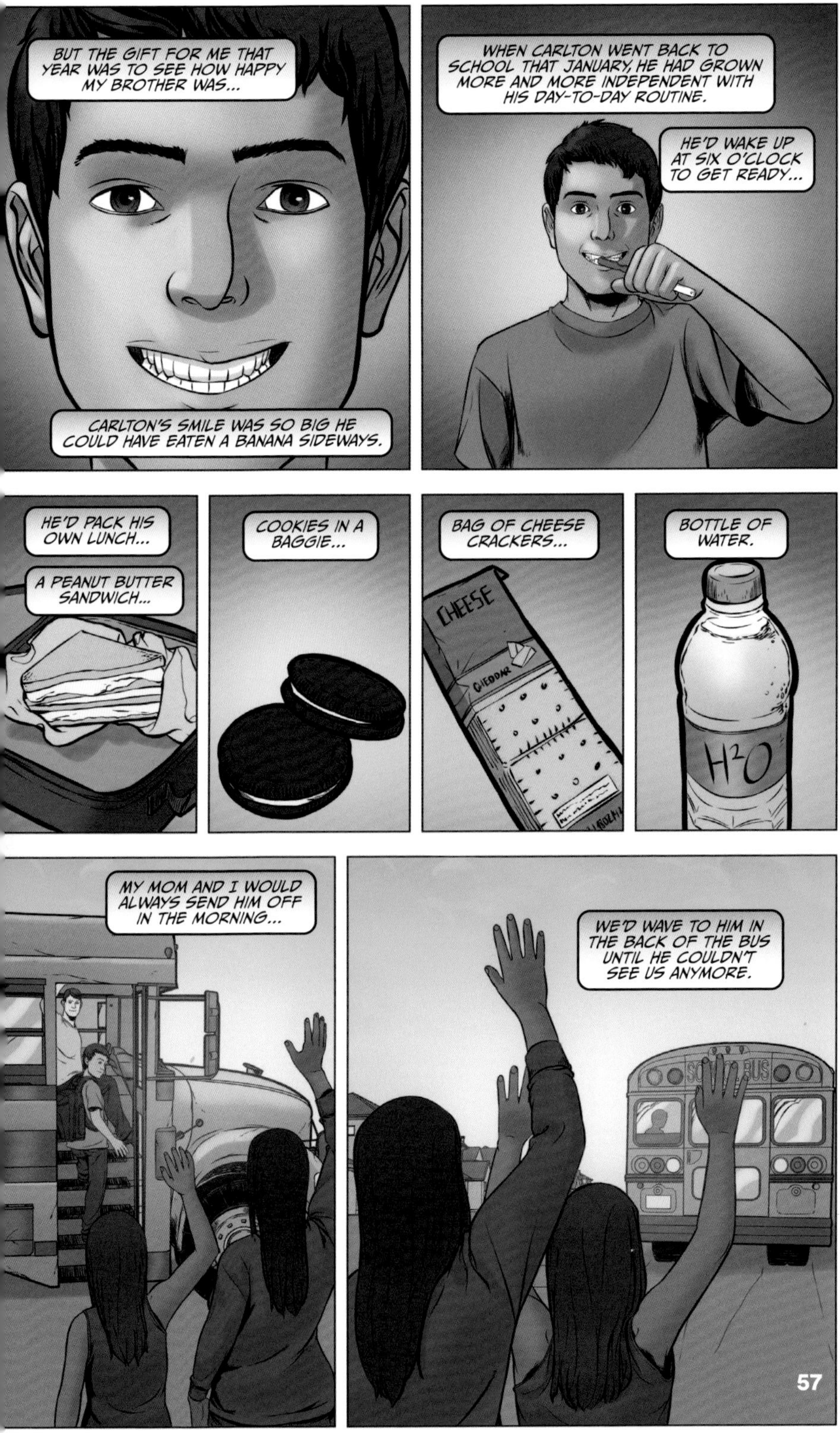
BUT THE GIFT FOR ME THAT YEAR WAS TO SEE HOW HAPPY MY BROTHER WAS...
CARLTON'S SMILE WAS SO BIG HE COULD HAVE EATEN A BANANA SIDEWAYS.
WHEN CARLTON WENT BACK TO SCHOOL THAT JANUARY, HE HAD GROWN MORE AND MORE INDEPENDENT WITH HIS DAY-TO-DAY ROUTINE.
HE'D WAKE UP AT SIX O'CLOCK TO GET READY...
HE'D PACK HIS OWN LUNCH...
A PEANUT BUTTER SANDWICH...
COOKIES IN A BAGGIE...
BAG OF CHEESE CRACKERS...
CHEESE
CHEDDAR
BOTTLE OF WATER.
H2O
MY MOM AND I WOULD ALWAYS SEND HIM OFF IN THE MORNING...
WE'D WAVE TO HIM IN THE BACK OF THE BUS UNTIL HE COULDN'T SEE US ANYMORE.

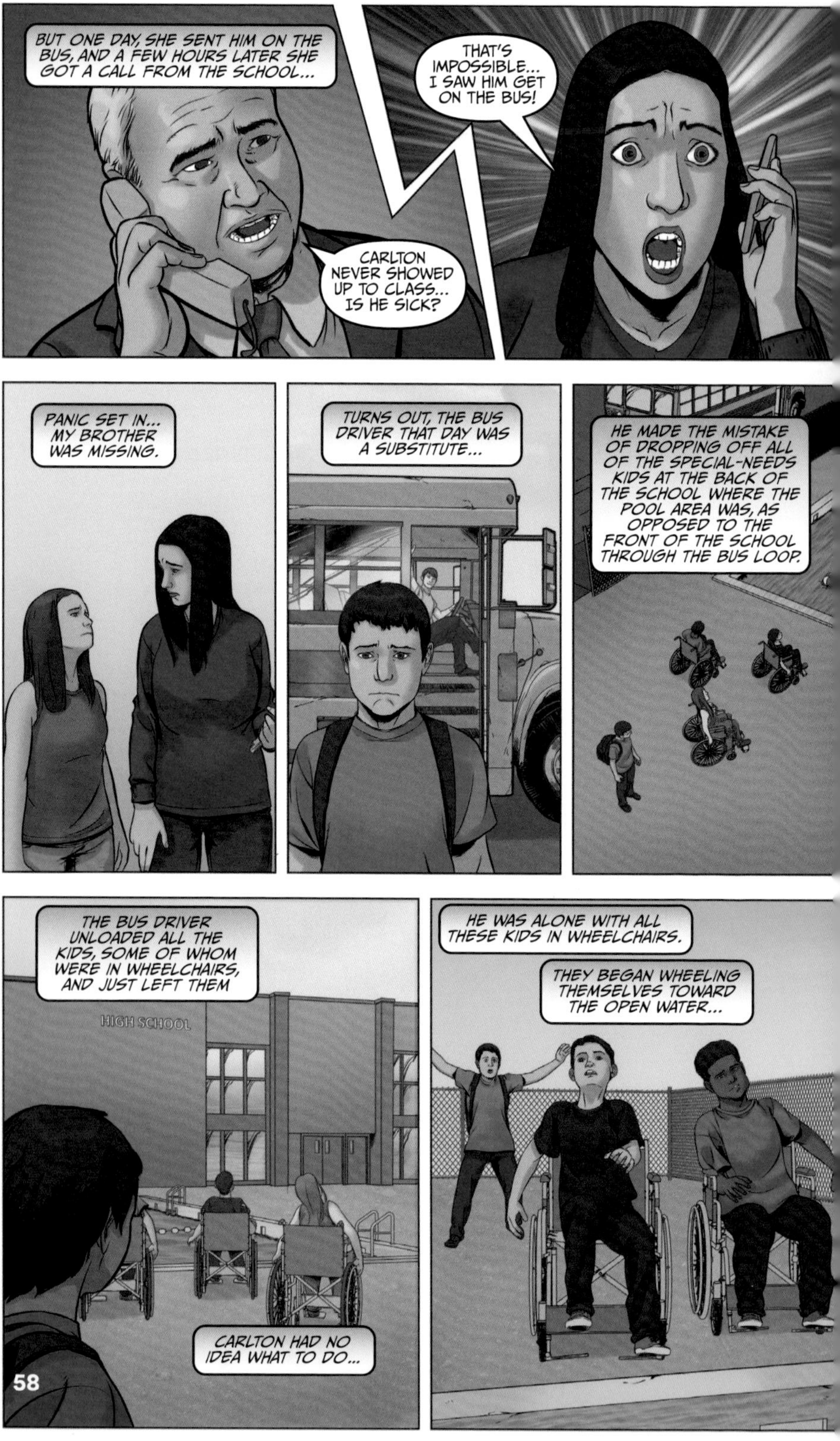
BUT ONE DAY, SHE SENT HIM ON THE BUS, AND A FEW HOURS LATER SHE GOT A CALL FROM THE SCHOOL...
CARLTON NEVER SHOWED UP TO CLASS... IS HE SICK?
THAT'S IMPOSSIBLE... I SAW HIM GET ON THE BUS!
PANIC SET IN... MY BROTHER WAS MISSING.
TURNS OUT, THE BUS DRIVER THAT DAY WAS A SUBSTITUTE...
HE MADE THE MISTAKE OF DROPPING OFF ALL OF THE SPECIAL-NEEDS KIDS AT THE BACK OF THE SCHOOL WHERE THE POOL AREA WAS, AS OPPOSED TO THE FRONT OF THE SCHOOL THROUGH THE BUS LOOP.
THE BUS DRIVER UNLOADED ALL THE KIDS, SOME OF WHOM WERE IN WHEELCHAIRS, AND JUST LEFT THEM
HIGH SCHOOL
CARLTON HAD NO IDEA WHAT TO DO...
HE WAS ALONE WITH ALL THESE KIDS IN WHEELCHAIRS.
THEY BEGAN WHEELING THEMSELVES TOWARD THE OPEN WATER...

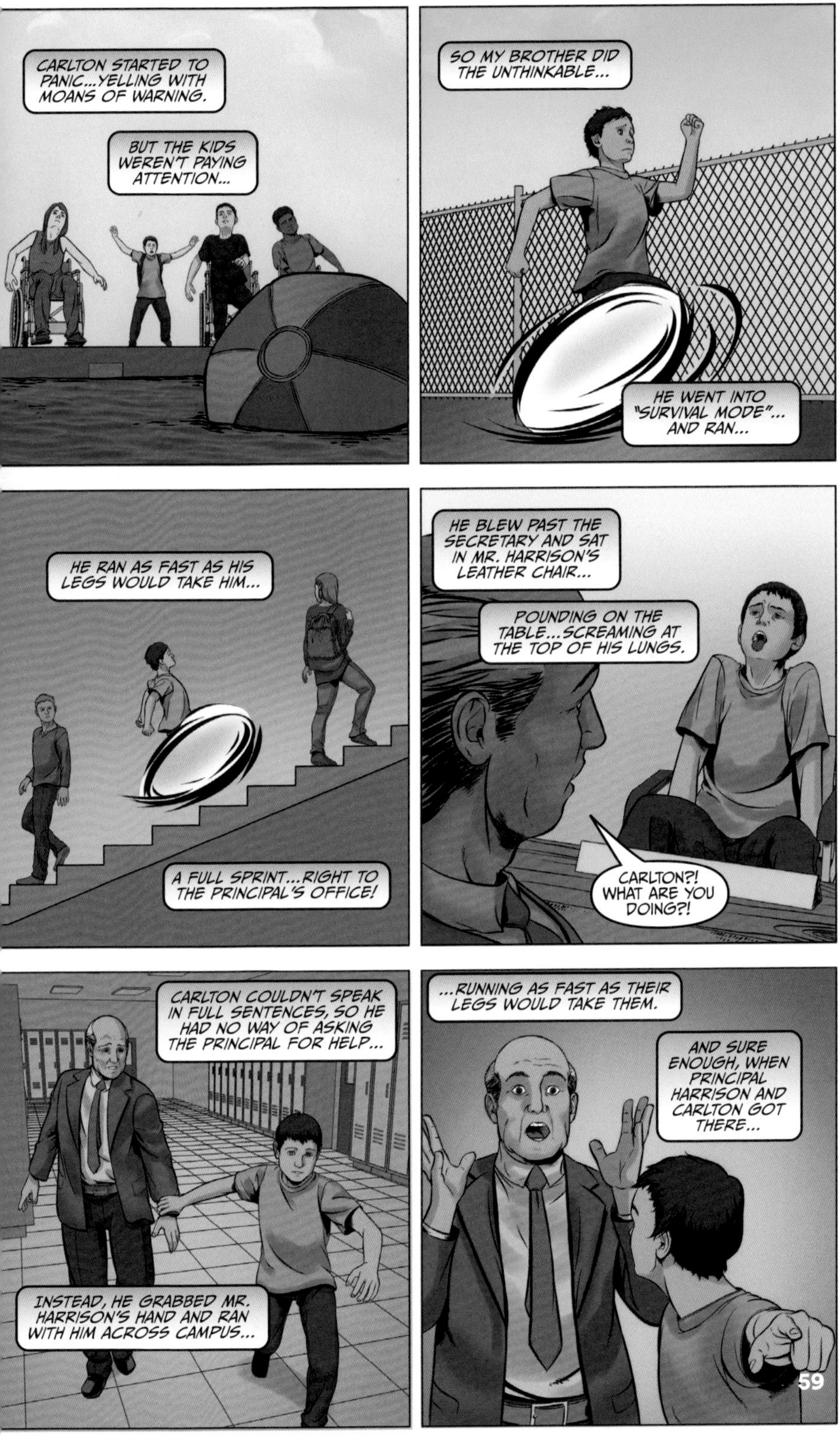

CARLTON STARTED TO PANIC...YELLING WITH MOANS OF WARNING.
BUT THE KIDS WEREN'T PAYING ATTENTION...
SO MY BROTHER DID THE UNTHINKABLE...
HE WENT INTO "SURVIVAL MODE"... AND RAN...
HE RAN AS FAST AS HIS LEGS WOULD TAKE HIM...
A FULL SPRINT...RIGHT TO THE PRINCIPAL'S OFFICE!
HE BLEW PAST THE SECRETARY AND SAT IN MR. HARRISON'S LEATHER CHAIR...
POUNDING ON THE TABLE...SCREAMING AT THE TOP OF HIS LUNGS.
CARLTON?! WHAT ARE YOU DOING?!
CARLTON COULDN'T SPEAK IN FULL SENTENCES, SO HE HAD NO WAY OF ASKING THE PRINCIPAL FOR HELP...
INSTEAD, HE GRABBED MR. HARRISON'S HAND AND RAN WITH HIM ACROSS CAMPUS...
...RUNNING AS FAST AS THEIR LEGS WOULD TAKE THEM.
AND SURE ENOUGH, WHEN PRINCIPAL HARRISON AND CARLTON GOT THERE...

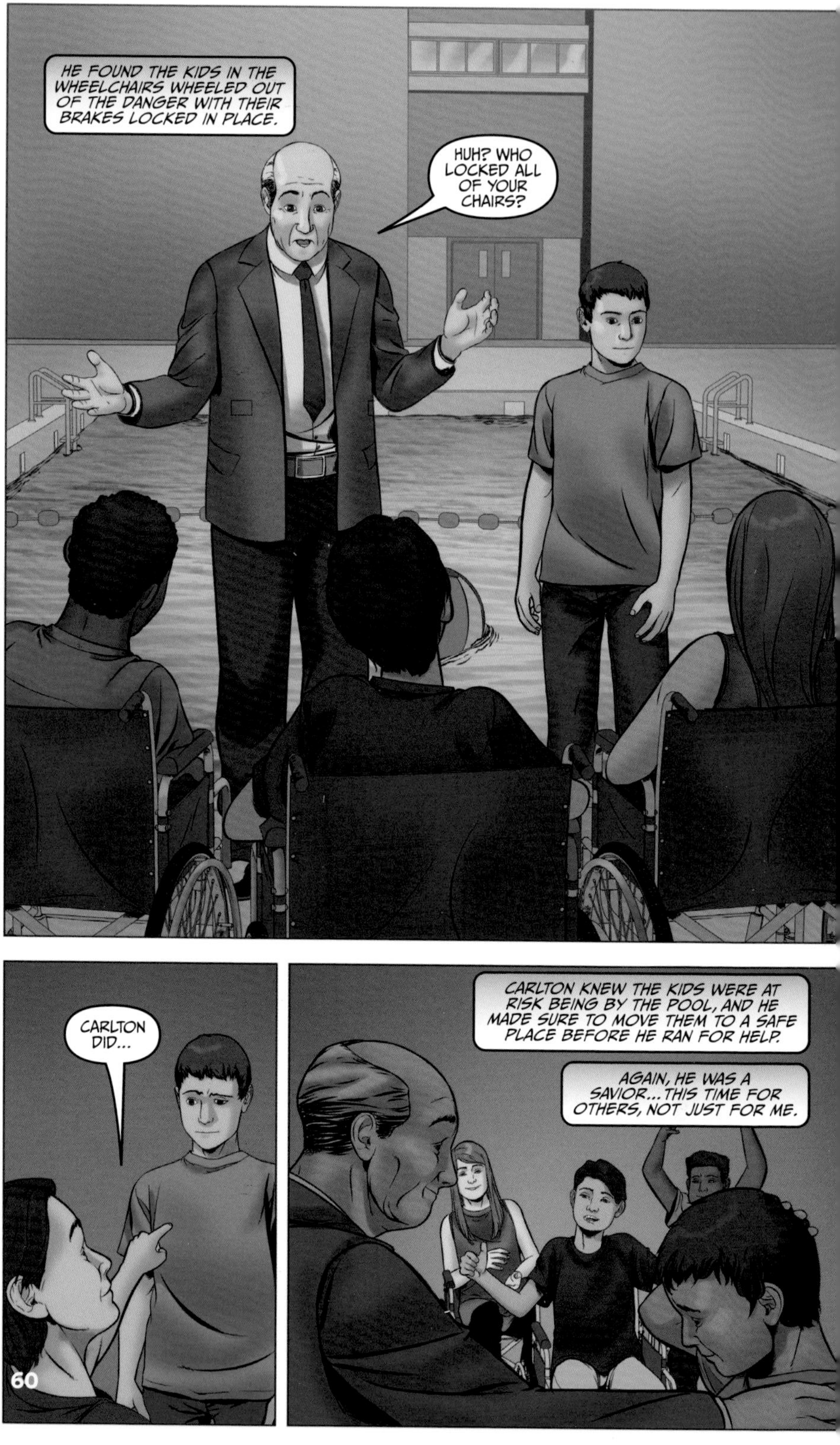
HE FOUND THE KIDS IN THE WHEELCHAIRS WHEELED OUT OF THE DANGER WITH THEIR BRAKES LOCKED IN PLACE.
HUH? WHO LOCKED ALL OF YOUR CHAIRS?
CARLTON DID...
CARLTON KNEW THE KIDS WERE AT RISK BEING BY THE POOL, AND HE MADE SURE TO MOVE THEM TO A SAFE PLACE BEFORE HE RAN FOR HELP.
AGAIN, HE WAS A SAVIOR...THIS TIME FOR OTHERS, NOT JUST FOR ME.

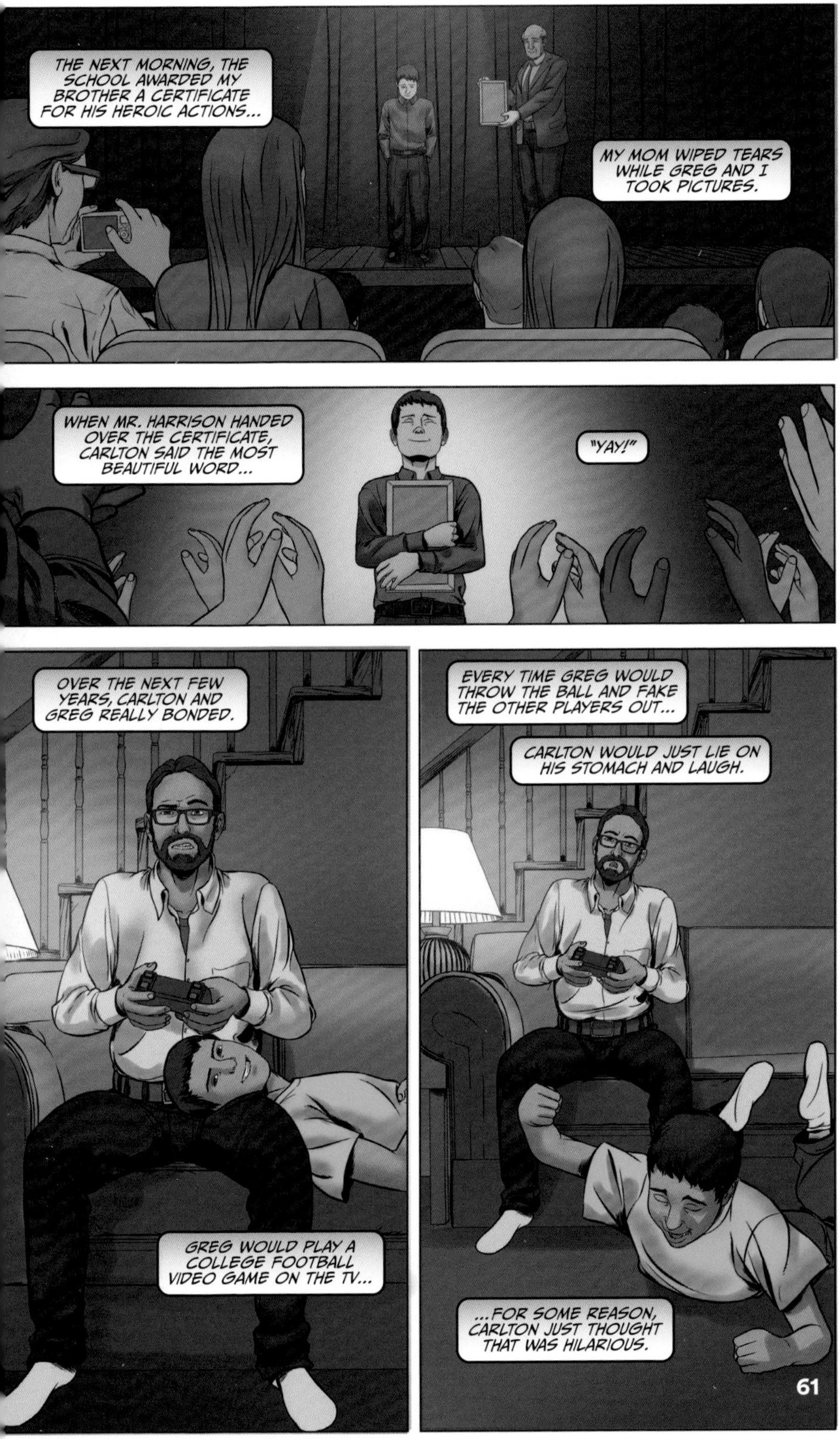
THE NEXT MORNING, THE SCHOOL AWARDED MY BROTHER A CERTIFICATE FOR HIS HEROIC ACTIONS...
MY MOM WIPED TEARS WHILE GREG AND I TOOK PICTURES.
WHEN MR. HARRISON HANDED OVER THE CERTIFICATE, CARLTON SAID THE MOST BEAUTIFUL WORD...
"YAY!"
OVER THE NEXT FEW YEARS, CARLTON AND GREG REALLY BONDED.
GREG WOULD PLAY A COLLEGE FOOTBALL VIDEO GAME ON THE TV...
EVERY TIME GREG WOULD THROW THE BALL AND FAKE THE OTHER PLAYERS OUT...
CARLTON WOULD JUST LIE ON HIS STOMACH AND LAUGH.
...FOR SOME REASON, CARLTON JUST THOUGHT THAT WAS HILARIOUS.

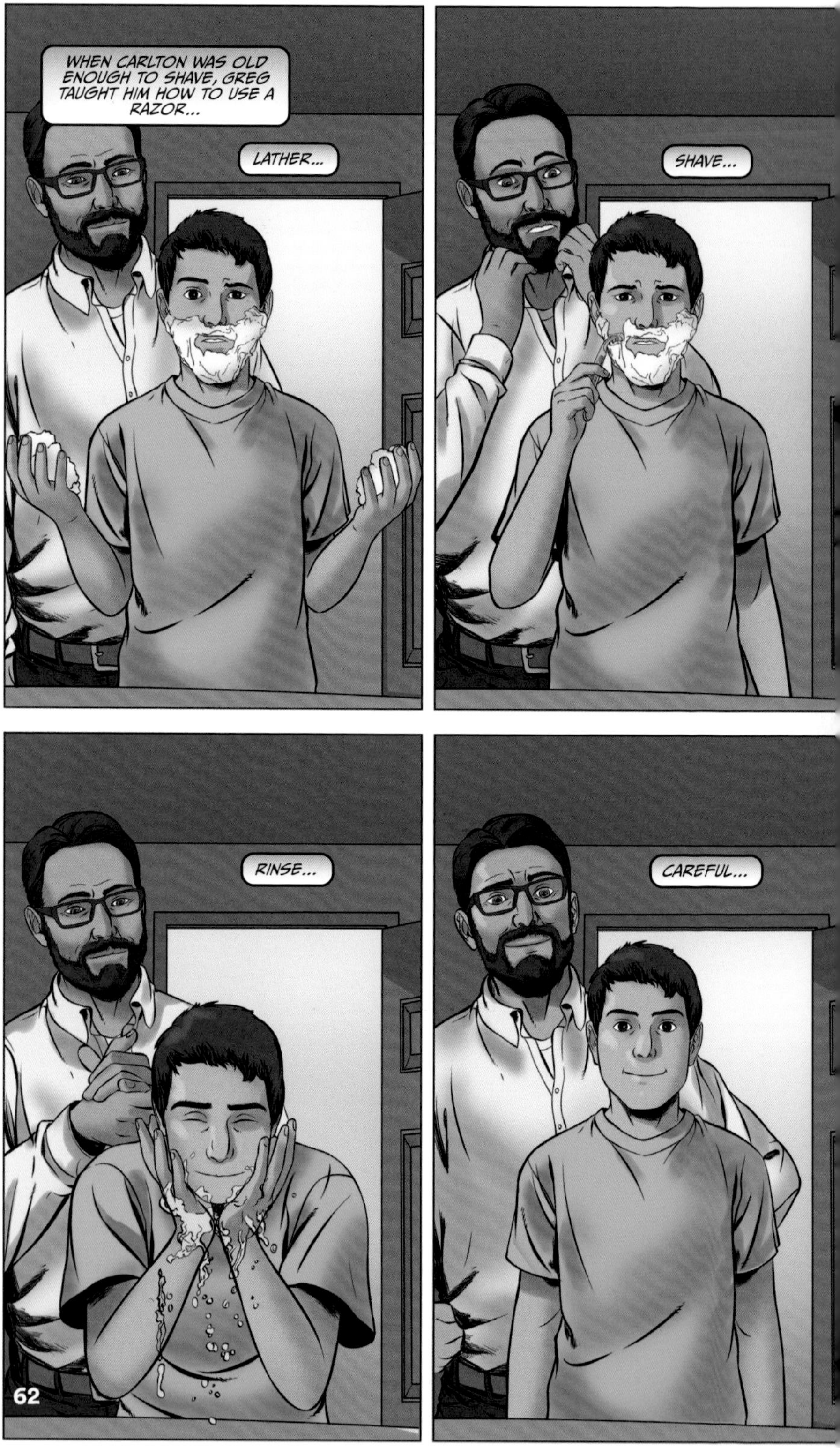
WHEN CARLTON WAS OLD ENOUGH TO SHAVE, GREG TAUGHT HIM HOW TO USE A RAZOR...
LATHER...
SHAVE...
RINSE...
CAREFUL...

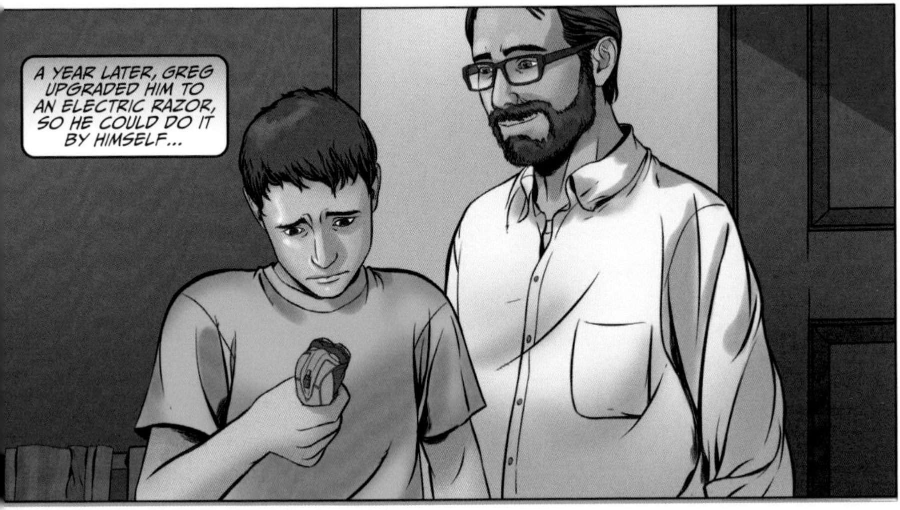
A YEAR LATER, GREG UPGRADED HIM TO AN ELECTRIC RAZOR, SO HE COULD DO IT BY HIMSELF...

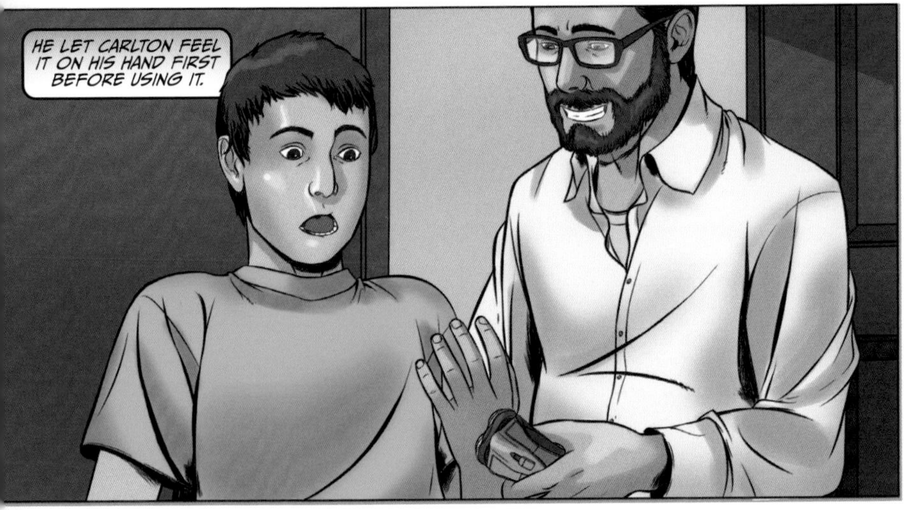
HE LET CARLTON FEEL IT ON HIS HAND FIRST BEFORE USING IT.

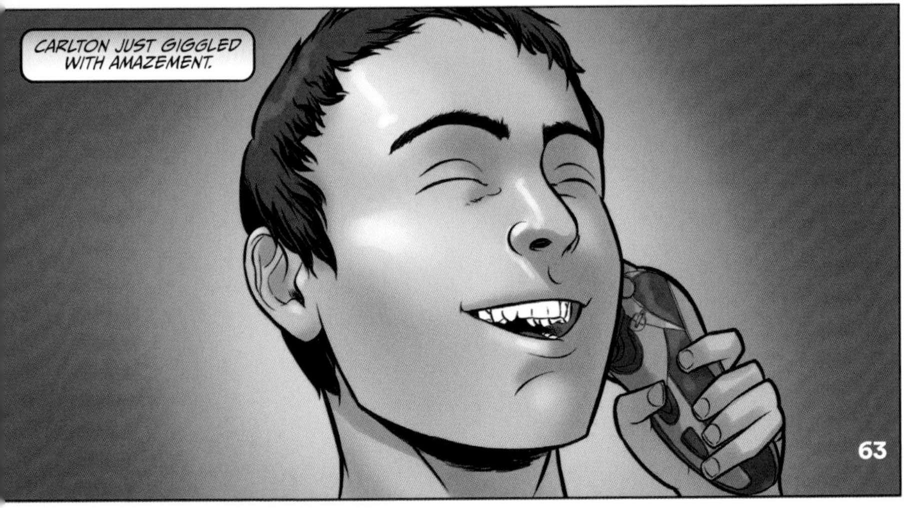
CARLTON JUST GIGGLED WITH AMAZEMENT.

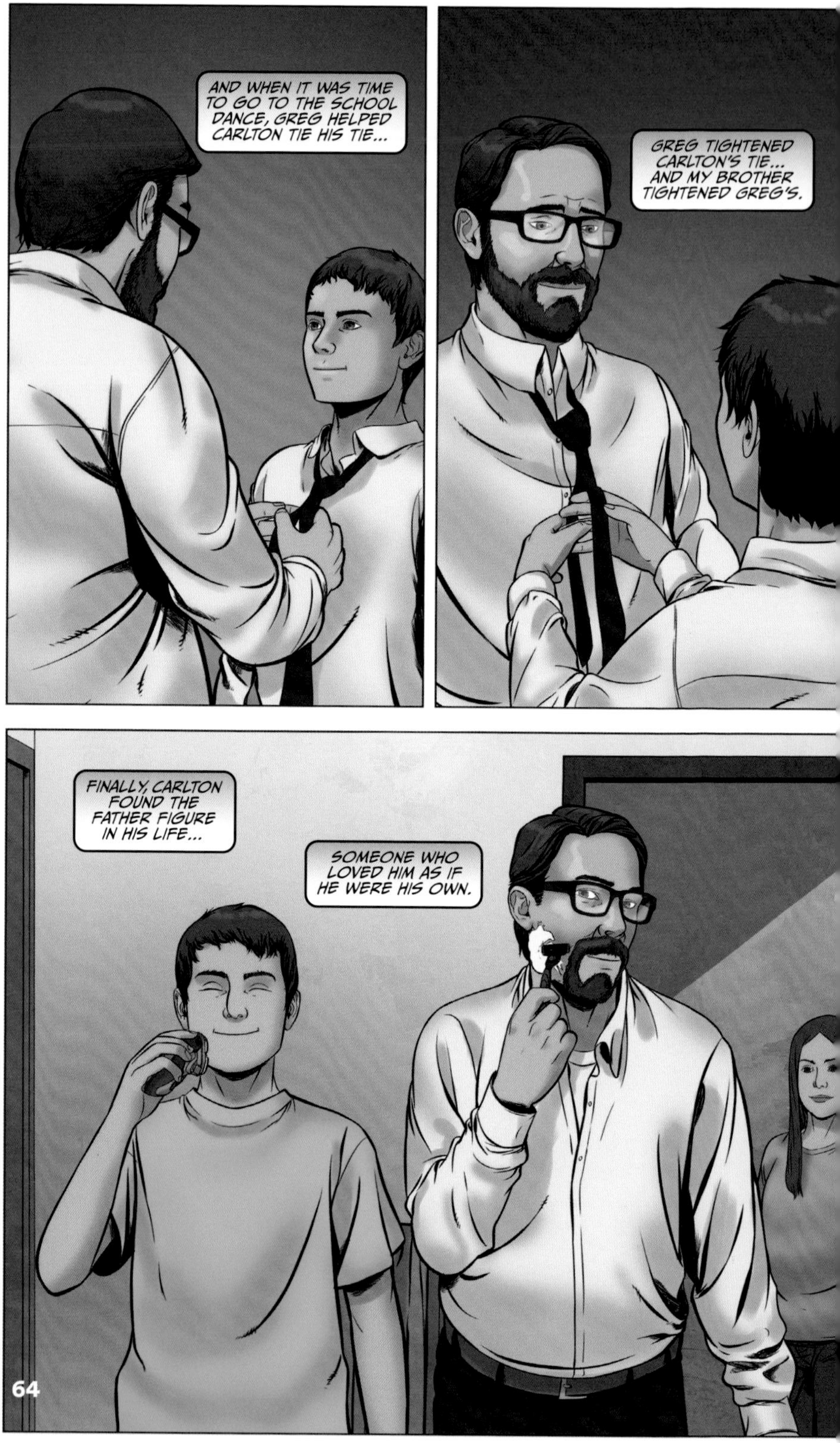
AND WHEN IT WAS TIME TO GO TO THE SCHOOL DANCE, GREG HELPED CARLTON TIE HIS TIE...
GREG TIGHTENED CARLTON'S TIE... AND MY BROTHER TIGHTENED GREG'S.
FINALLY, CARLTON FOUND THE FATHER FIGURE IN HIS LIFE...
SOMEONE WHO LOVED HIM AS IF HE WERE HIS OWN.

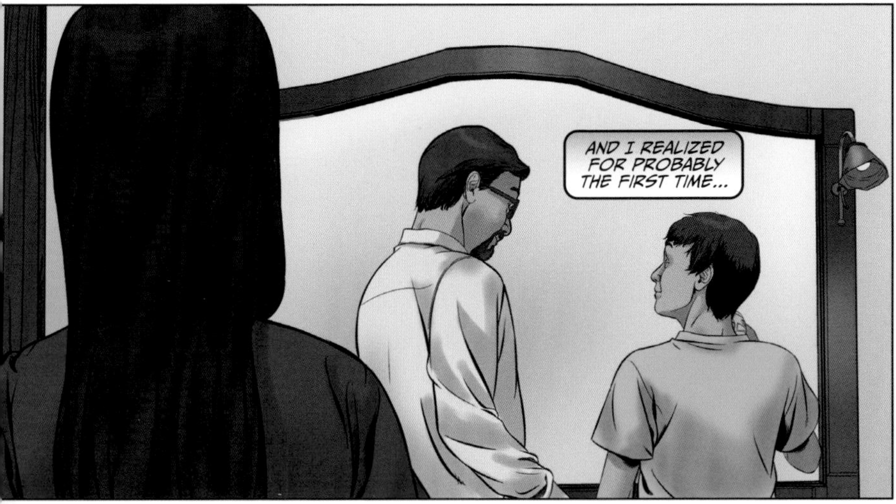
AND I REALIZED FOR PROBABLY THE FIRST TIME...

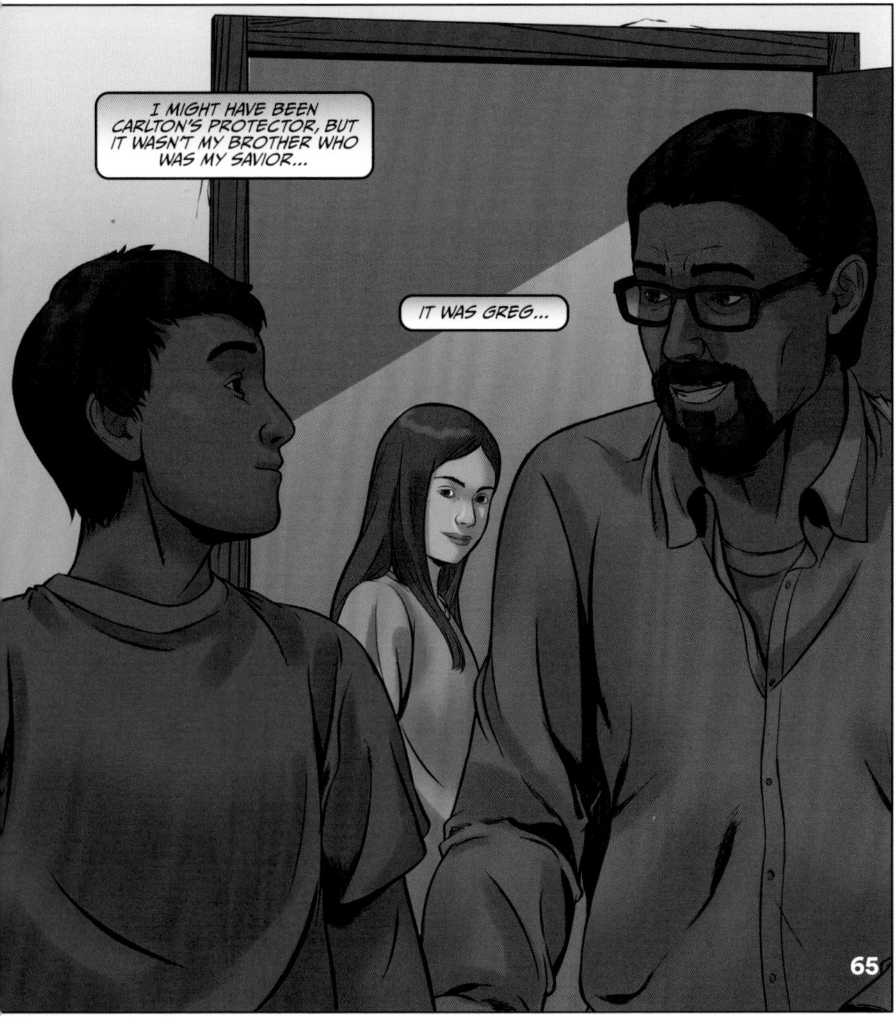
I MIGHT HAVE BEEN CARLTON'S PROTECTOR, BUT IT WASN'T MY BROTHER WHO WAS MY SAVIOR...
IT WAS GREG...

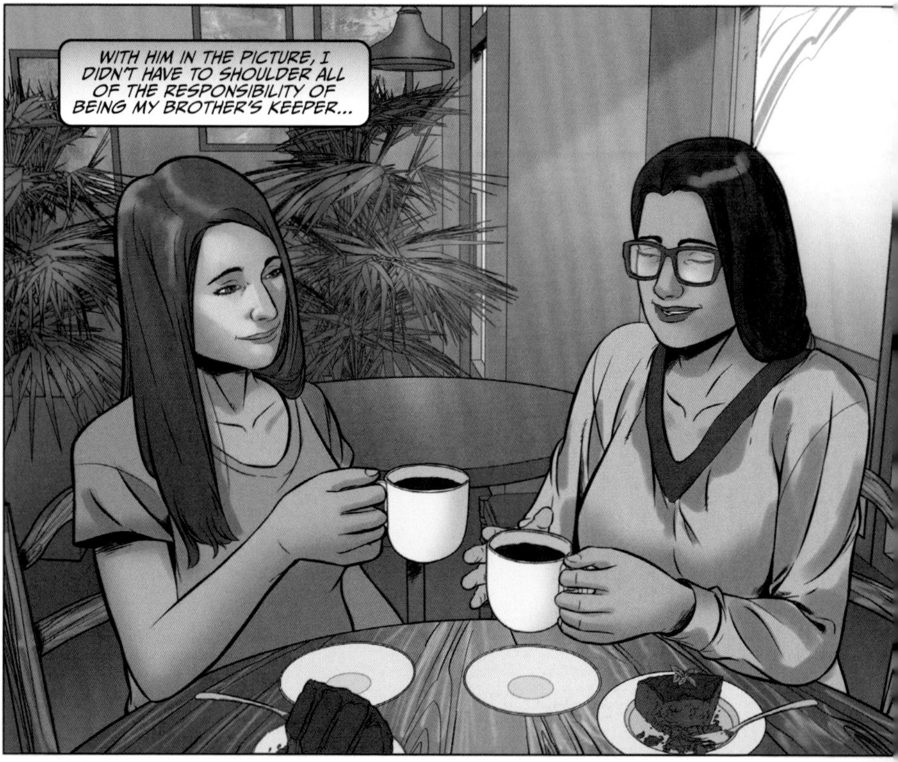
WITH HIM IN THE PICTURE, I DIDN'T HAVE TO SHOULDER ALL OF THE RESPONSIBILITY OF BEING MY BROTHER'S KEEPER...

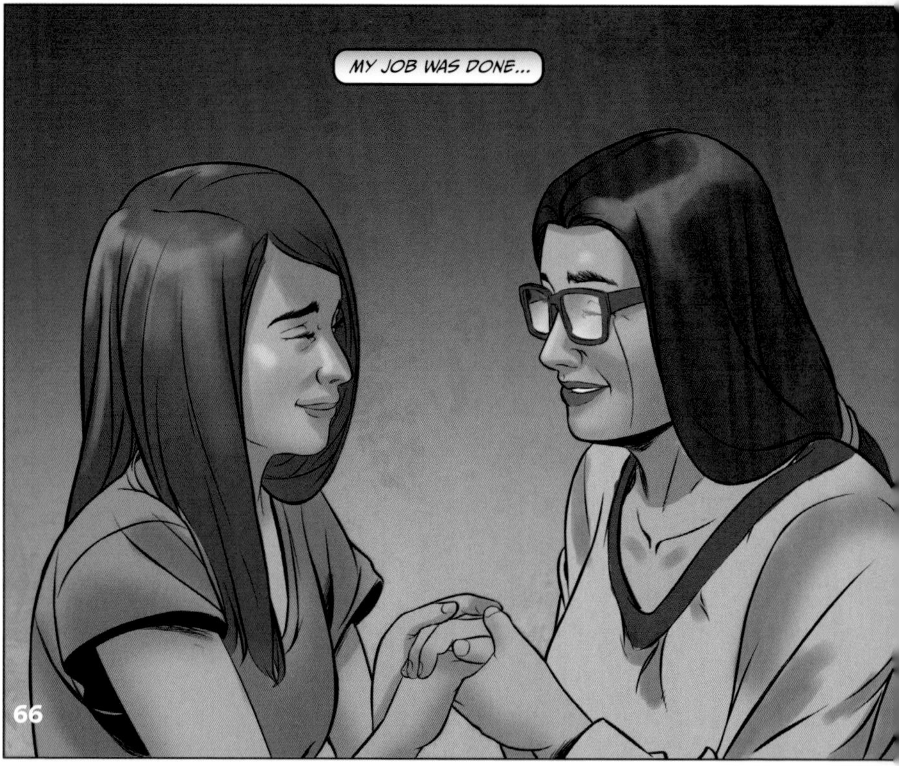
MY JOB WAS DONE...

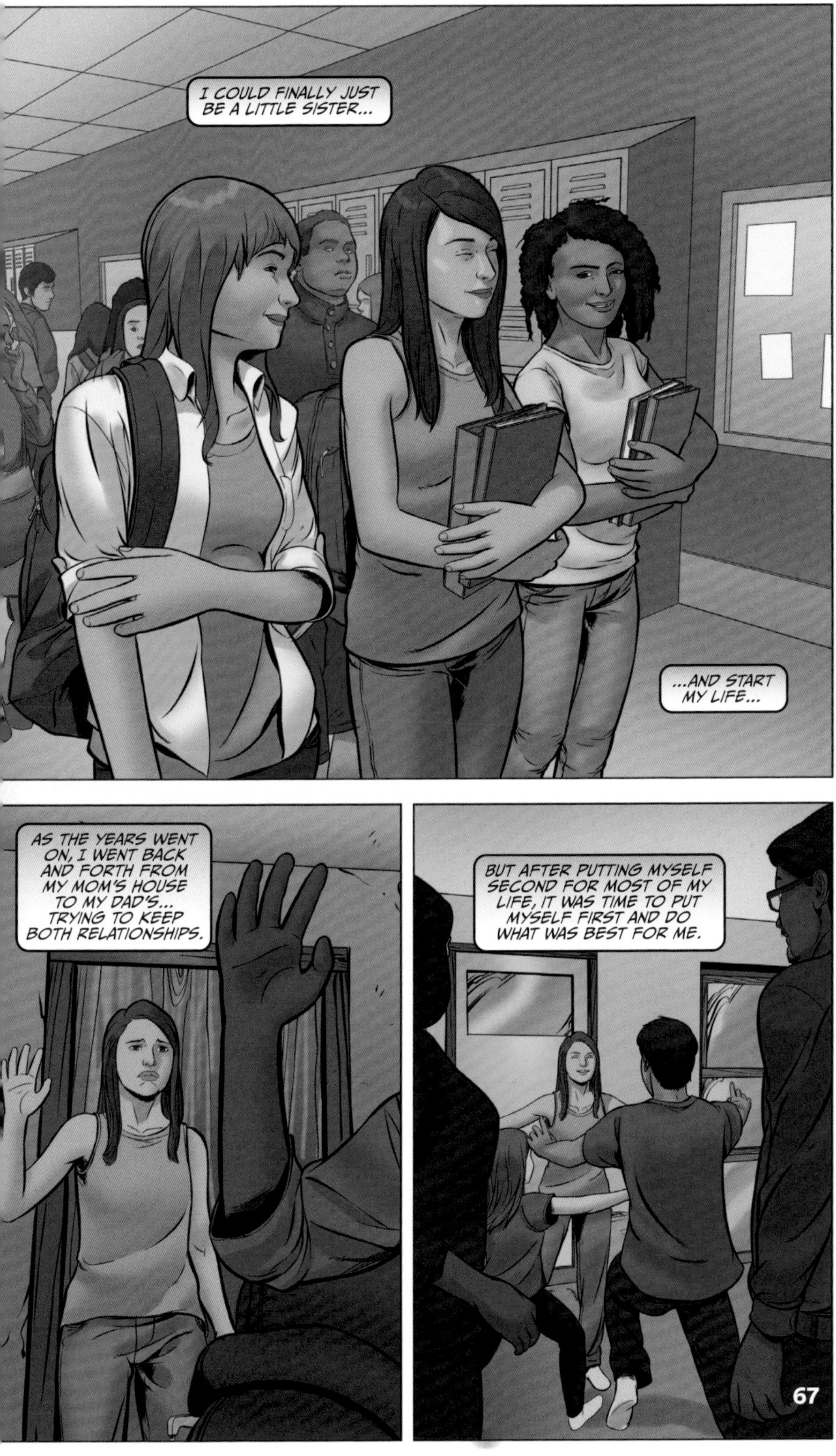
I COULD FINALLY JUST BE A LITTLE SISTER...
...AND START MY LIFE...
AS THE YEARS WENT ON, I WENT BACK AND FORTH FROM MY MOM'S HOUSE TO MY DAD'S... TRYING TO KEEP BOTH RELATIONSHIPS.
BUT AFTER PUTTING MYSELF SECOND FOR MOST OF MY LIFE, IT WAS TIME TO PUT MYSELF FIRST AND DO WHAT WAS BEST FOR ME.

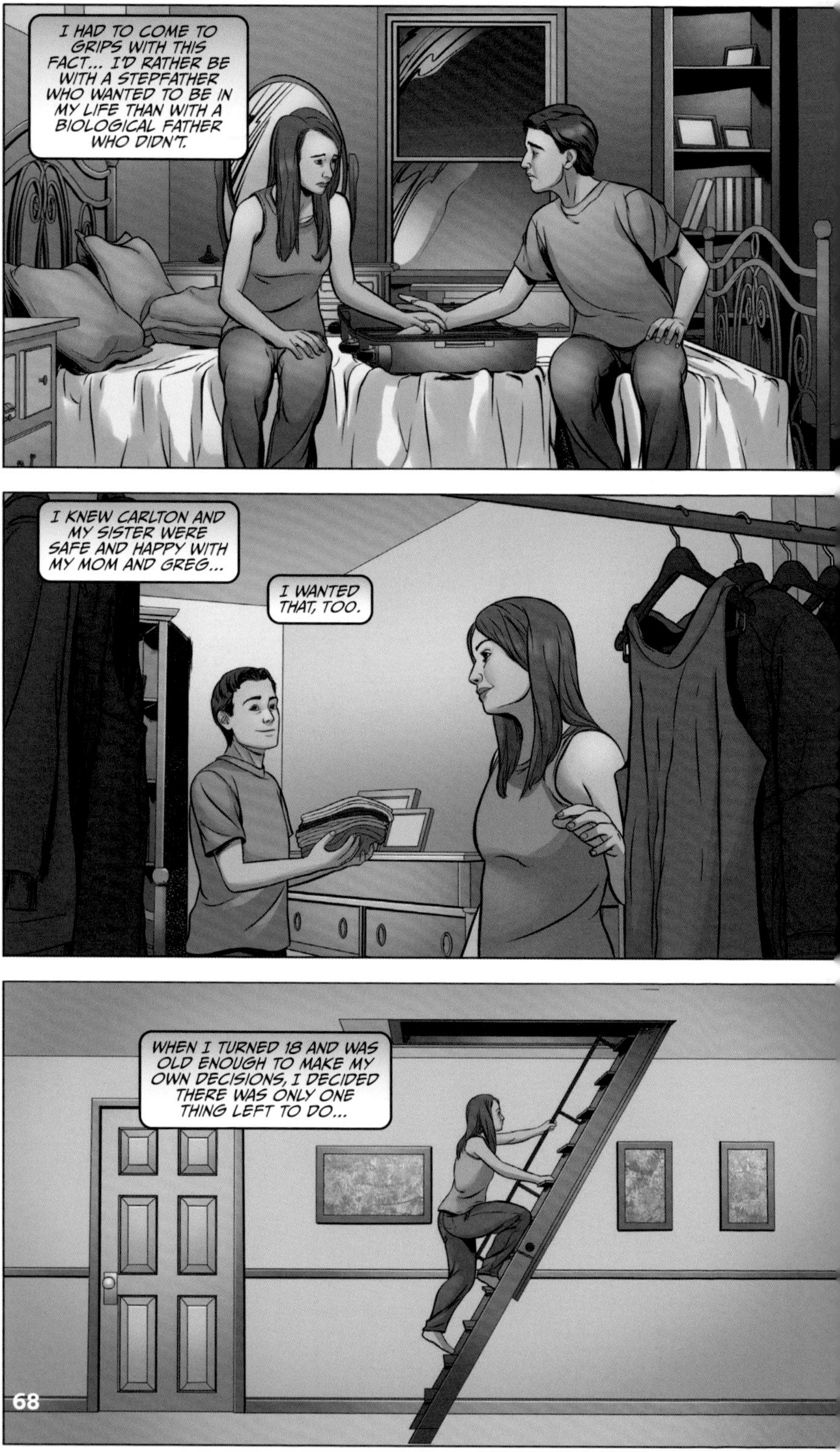
I HAD TO COME TO GRIPS WITH THIS FACT... I'D RATHER BE WITH A STEPFATHER WHO WANTED TO BE IN MY LIFE THAN WITH A BIOLOGICAL FATHER WHO DIDN'T.
I KNEW CARLTON AND MY SISTER WERE SAFE AND HAPPY WITH MY MOM AND GREG...
I WANTED THAT, TOO.
WHEN I TURNED 18 AND WAS OLD ENOUGH TO MAKE MY OWN DECISIONS, I DECIDED THERE WAS ONLY ONE THING LEFT TO DO...

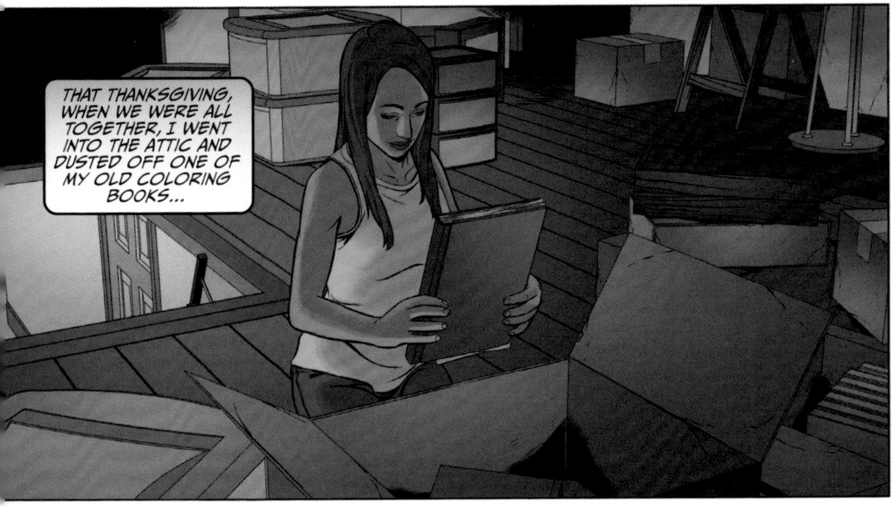
THAT THANKSGIVING, WHEN WE WERE ALL TOGETHER, I WENT INTO THE ATTIC AND DUSTED OFF ONE OF MY OLD COLORING BOOKS...

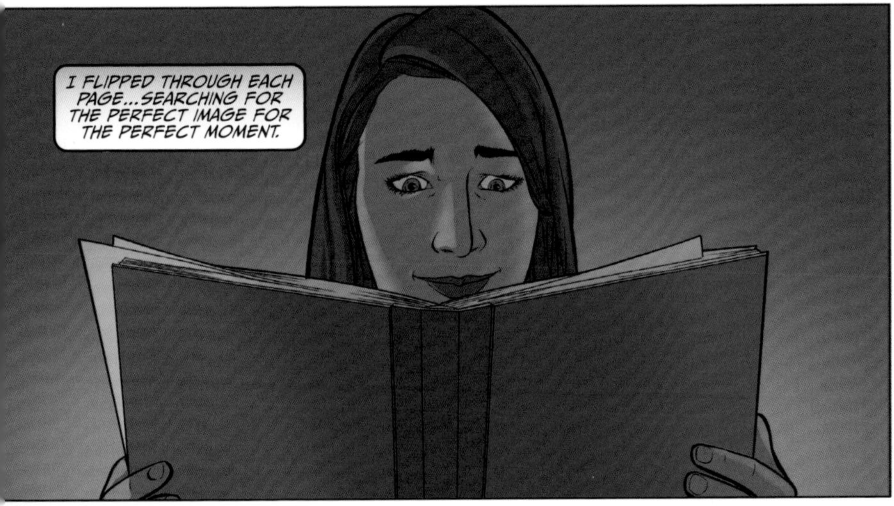
I FLIPPED THROUGH EACH PAGE...SEARCHING FOR THE PERFECT IMAGE FOR THE PERFECT MOMENT.

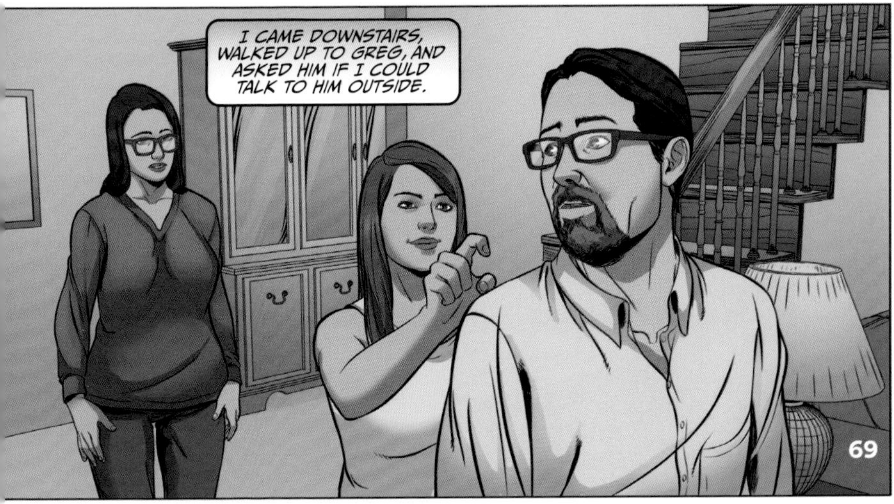
I CAME DOWNSTAIRS, WALKED UP TO GREG, AND ASKED HIM IF I COULD TALK TO HIM OUTSIDE.

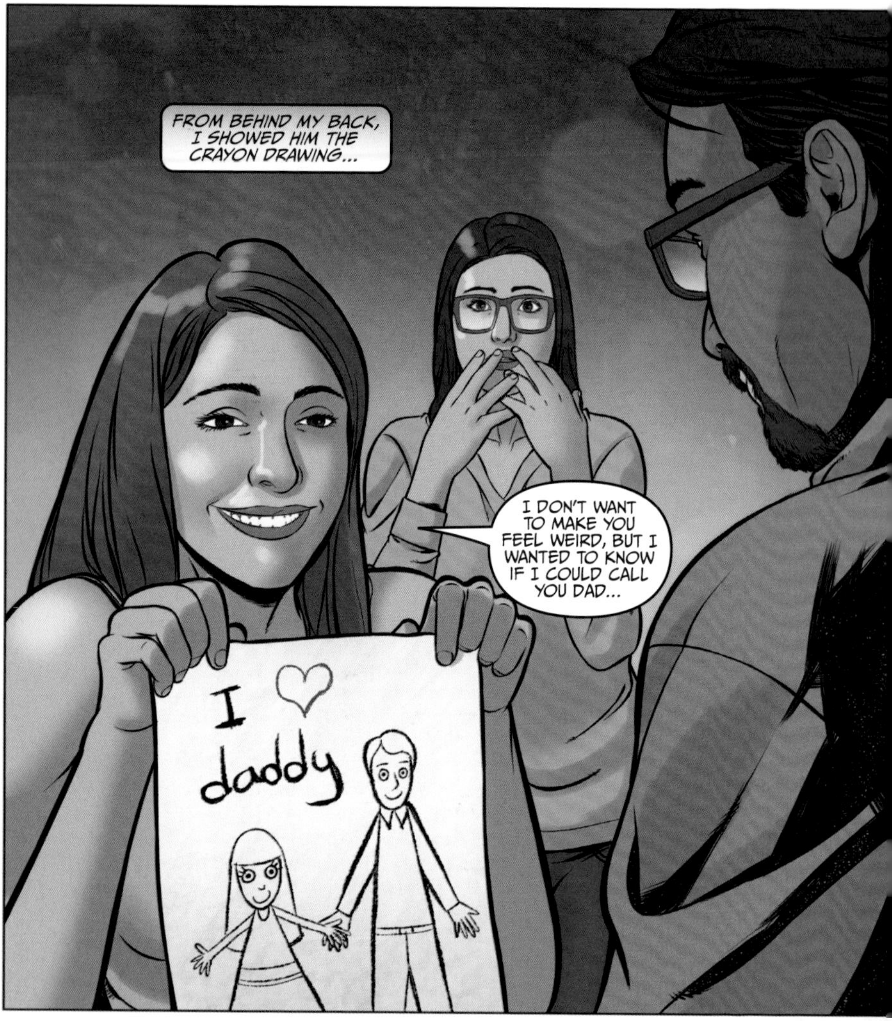
FROM BEHIND MY BACK, I SHOWED HIM THE CRAYON DRAWING...
I DON'T WANT TO MAKE YOU FEEL WEIRD, BUT I WANTED TO KNOW IF I COULD CALL YOU DAD...
I ♡ daddy
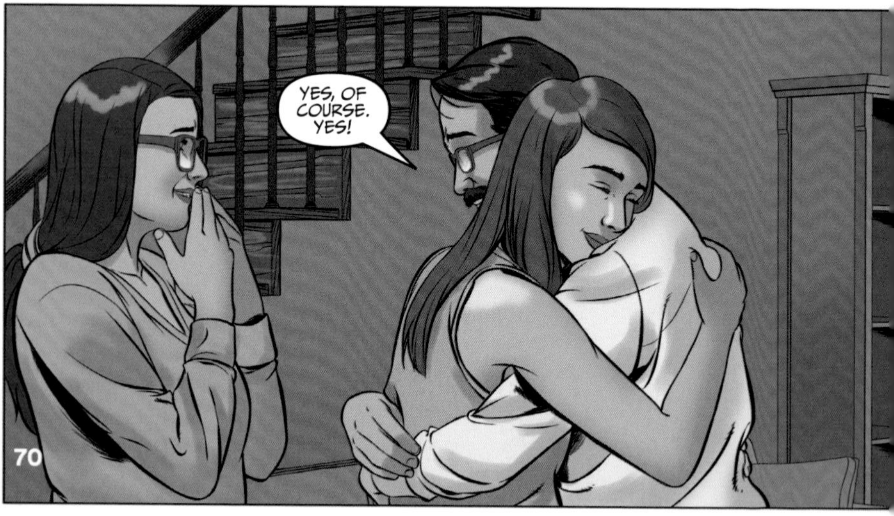
YES, OF COURSE. YES!

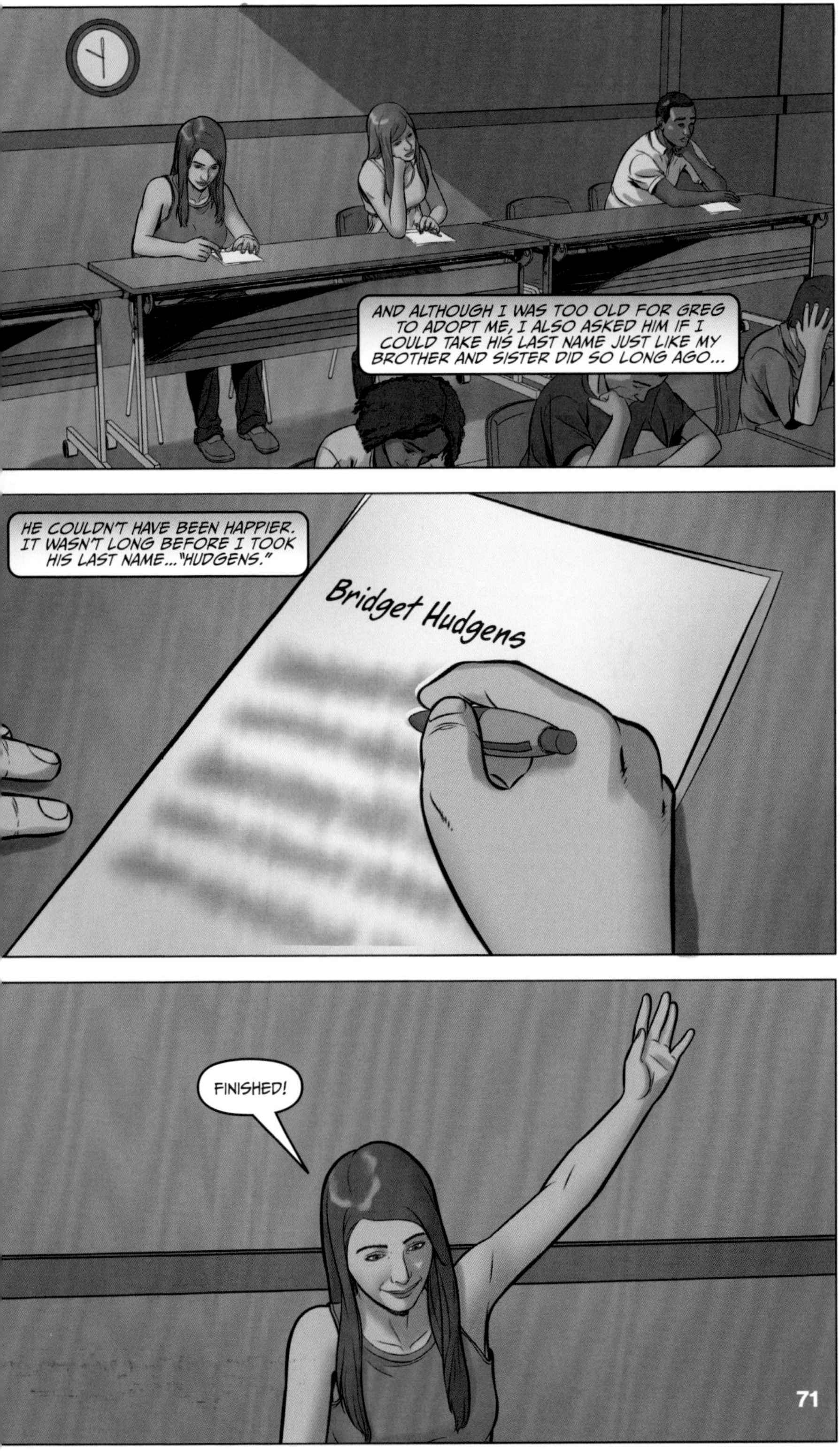
AND ALTHOUGH I WAS TOO OLD FOR GREG TO ADOPT ME, I ALSO ASKED HIM IF I COULD TAKE HIS LAST NAME JUST LIKE MY BROTHER AND SISTER DID SO LONG AGO...
HE COULDN'T HAVE BEEN HAPPIER. IT WASN'T LONG BEFORE I TOOK HIS LAST NAME..."HUDGENS."
Bridget Hudgens
FINISHED!

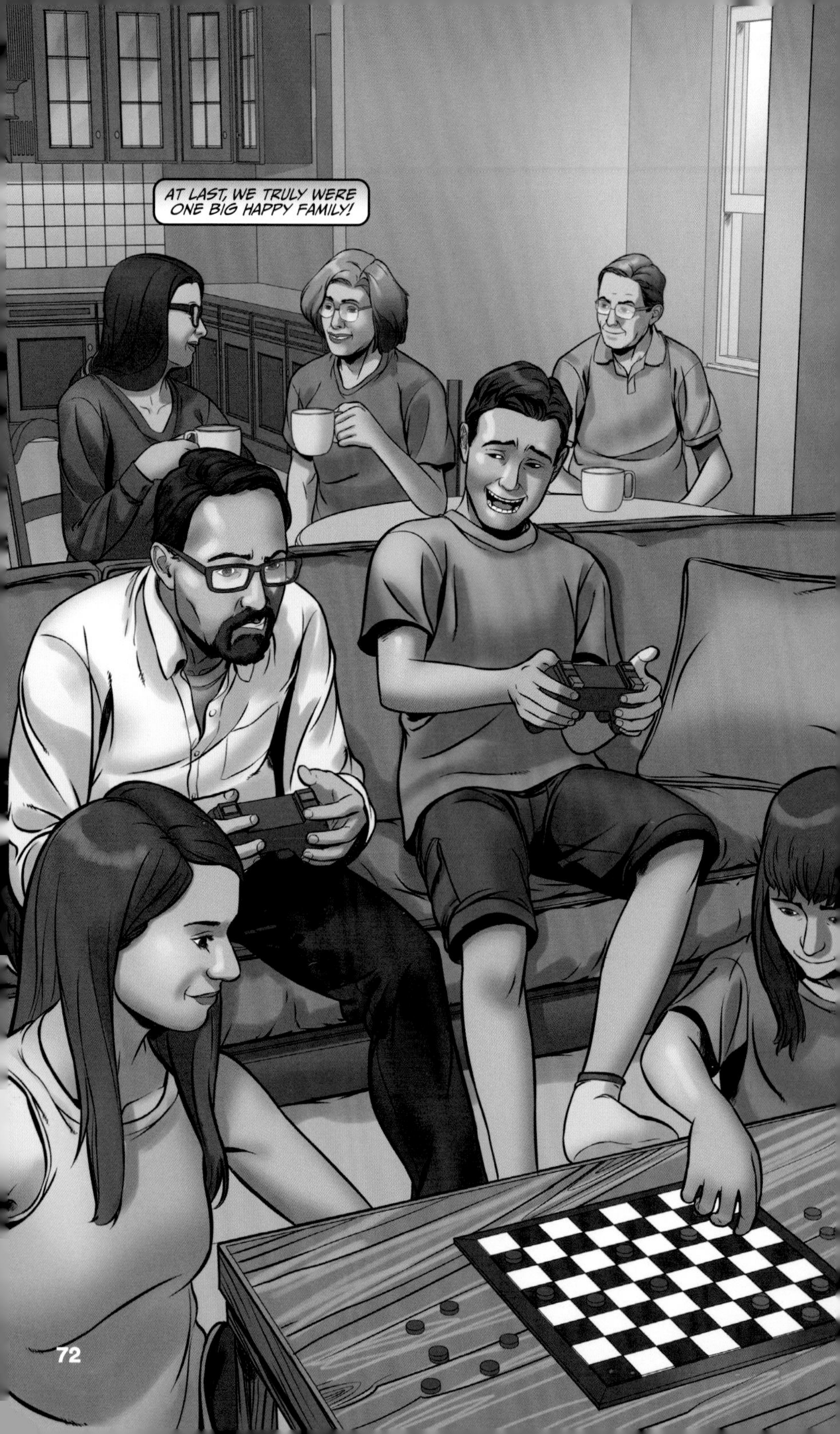
AT LAST, WE TRULY WERE ONE BIG HAPPY FAMILY!

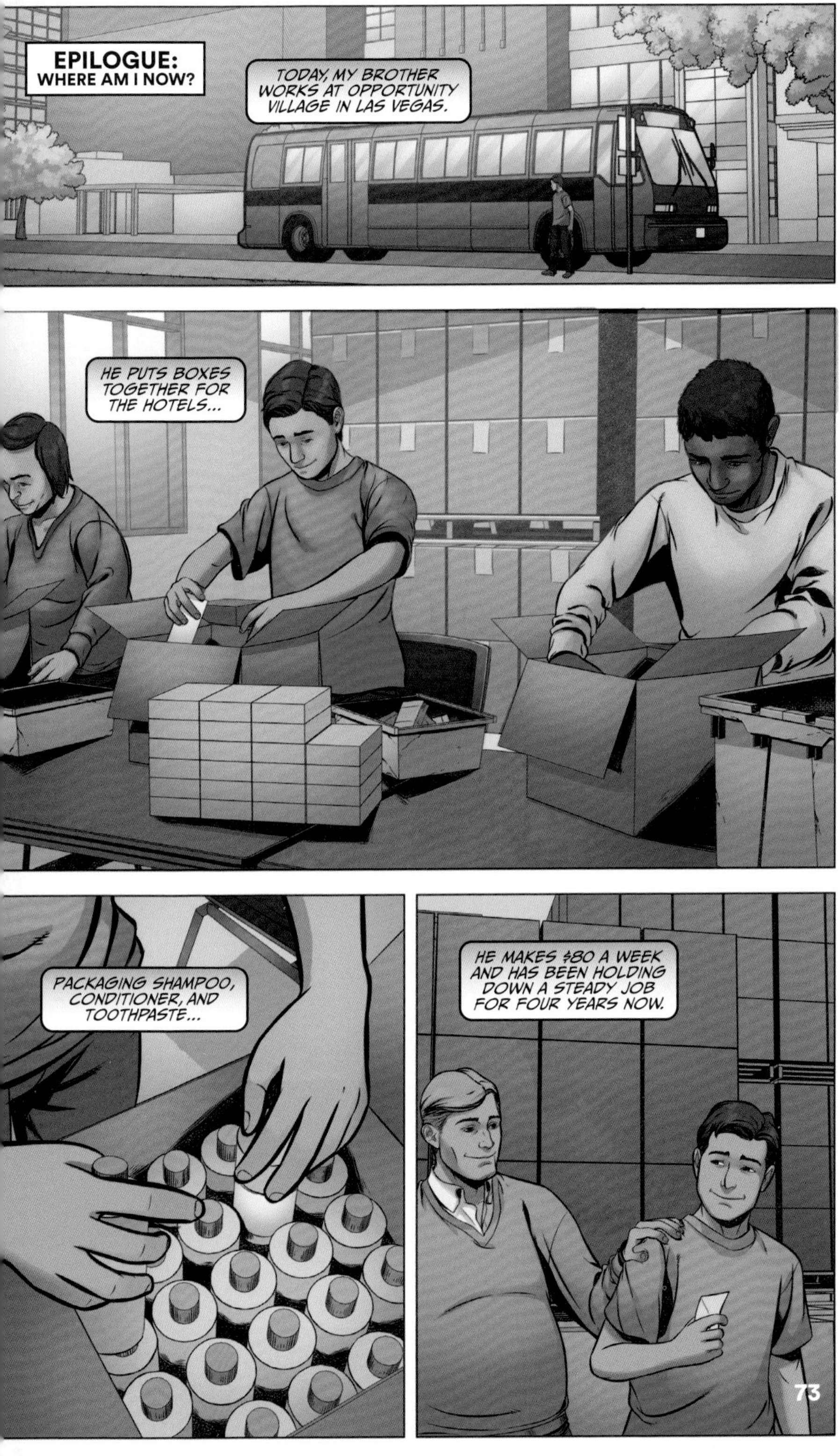
EPILOGUE: WHERE AM I NOW?
TODAY, MY BROTHER WORKS AT OPPORTUNITY VILLAGE IN LAS VEGAS.
HE PUTS BOXES TOGETHER FOR THE HOTELS...
PACKAGING SHAMPOO, CONDITIONER, AND TOOTHPASTE...
HE MAKES $80 A WEEK AND HAS BEEN HOLDING DOWN A STEADY JOB FOR FOUR YEARS NOW.

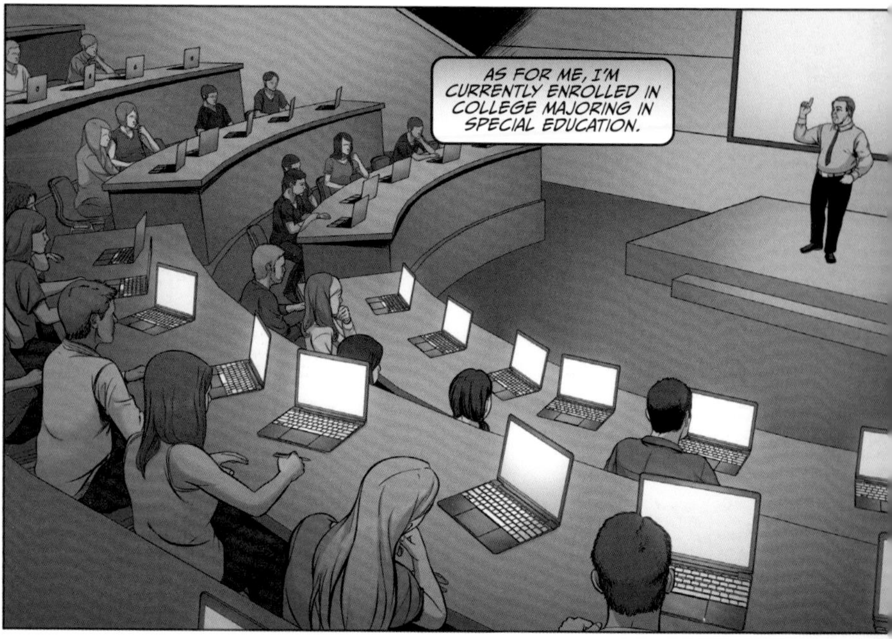
AS FOR ME, I'M CURRENTLY ENROLLED IN COLLEGE MAJORING IN SPECIAL EDUCATION.

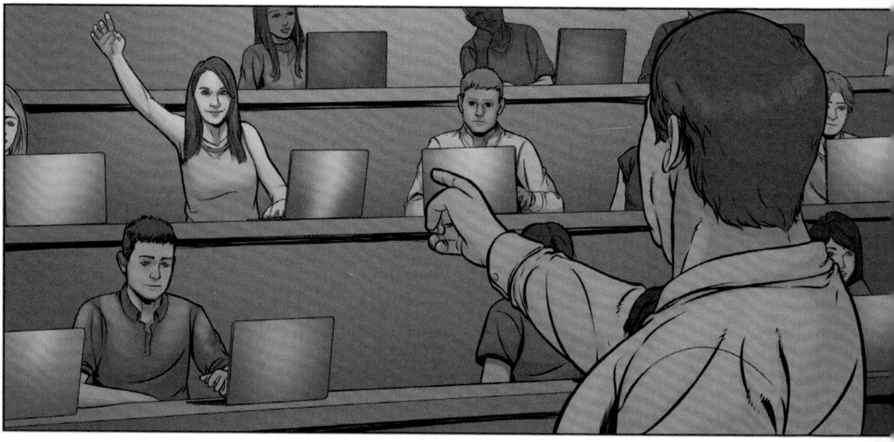

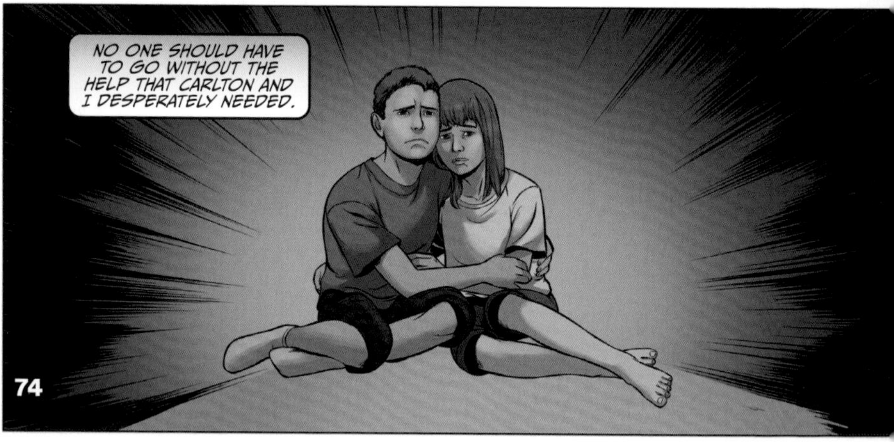
NO ONE SHOULD HAVE TO GO WITHOUT THE HELP THAT CARLTON AND I DESPERATELY NEEDED.

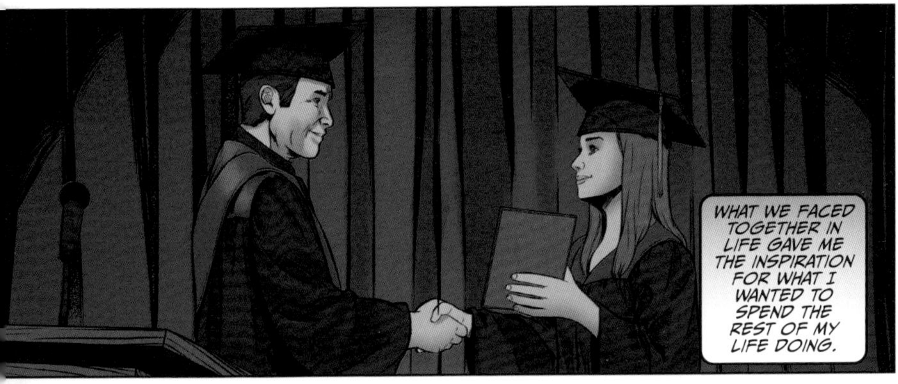
WHAT WE FACED TOGETHER IN LIFE GAVE ME THE INSPIRATION FOR WHAT I WANTED TO SPEND THE REST OF MY LIFE DOING.

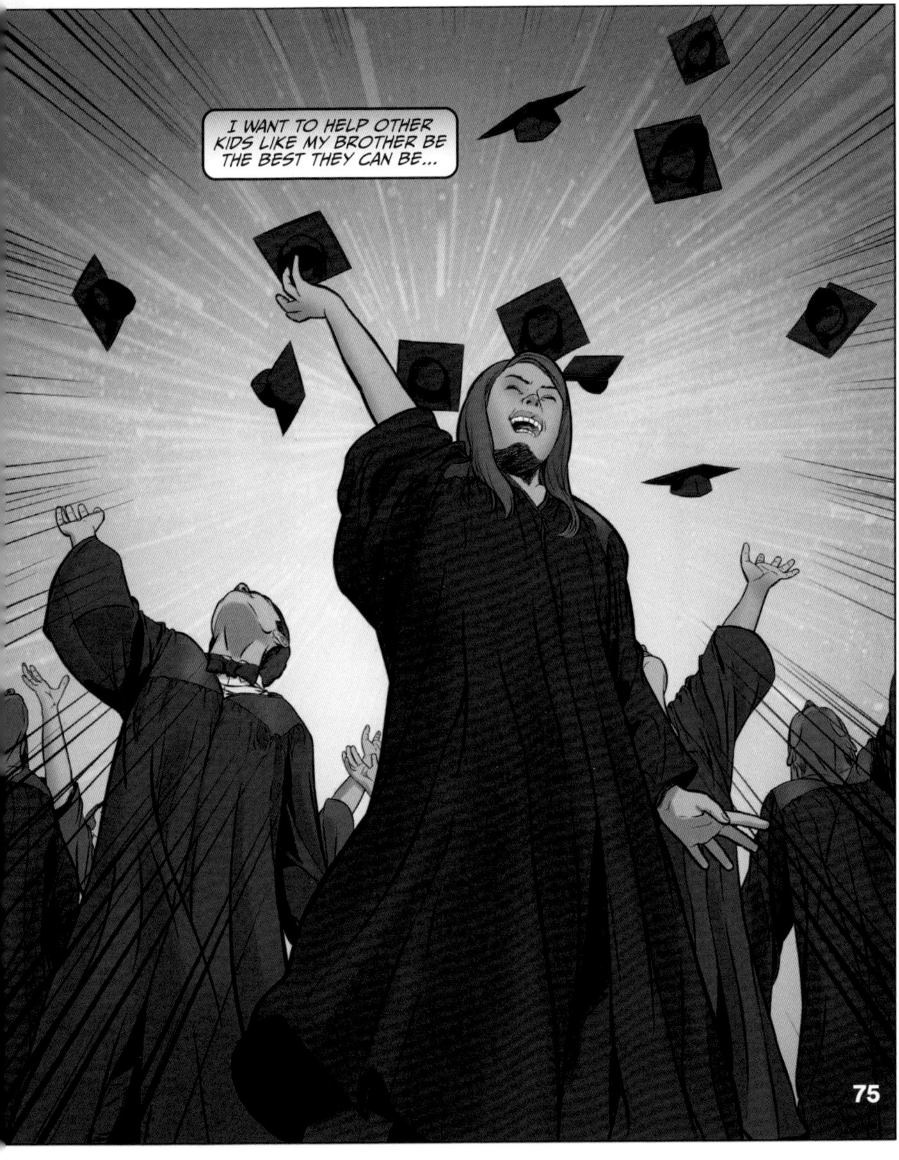
I WANT TO HELP OTHER KIDS LIKE MY BROTHER BE THE BEST THEY CAN BE...

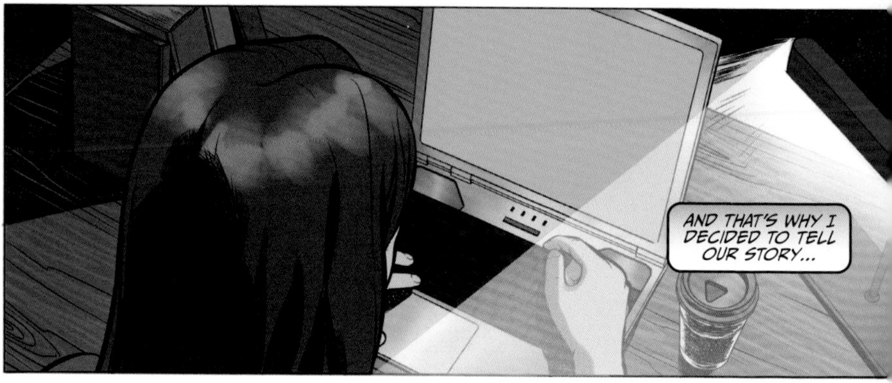
AND THAT'S WHY I DECIDED TO TELL OUR STORY...

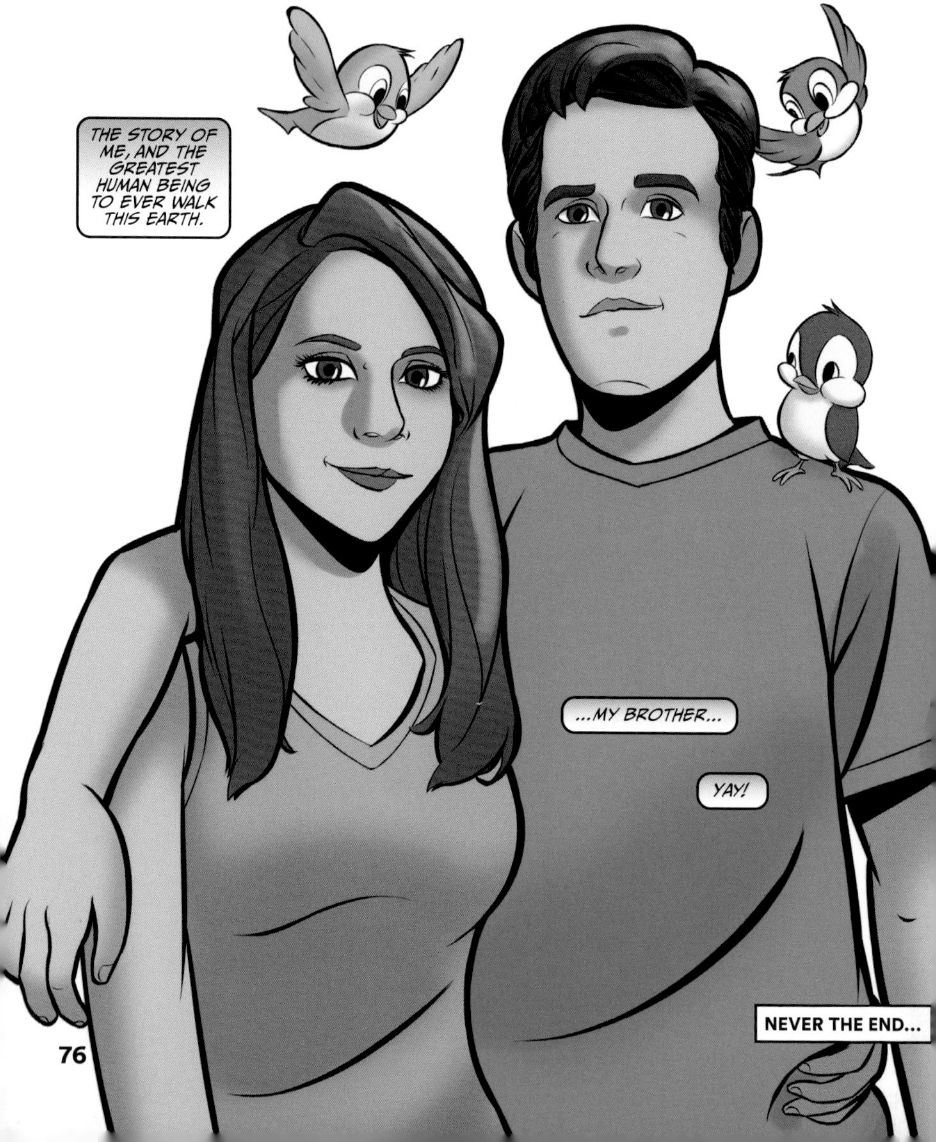
THE STORY OF ME, AND THE GREATEST HUMAN BEING TO EVER WALK THIS EARTH.
...MY BROTHER...
YAY!
NEVER THE END...

ABOUT THE AUTHOR

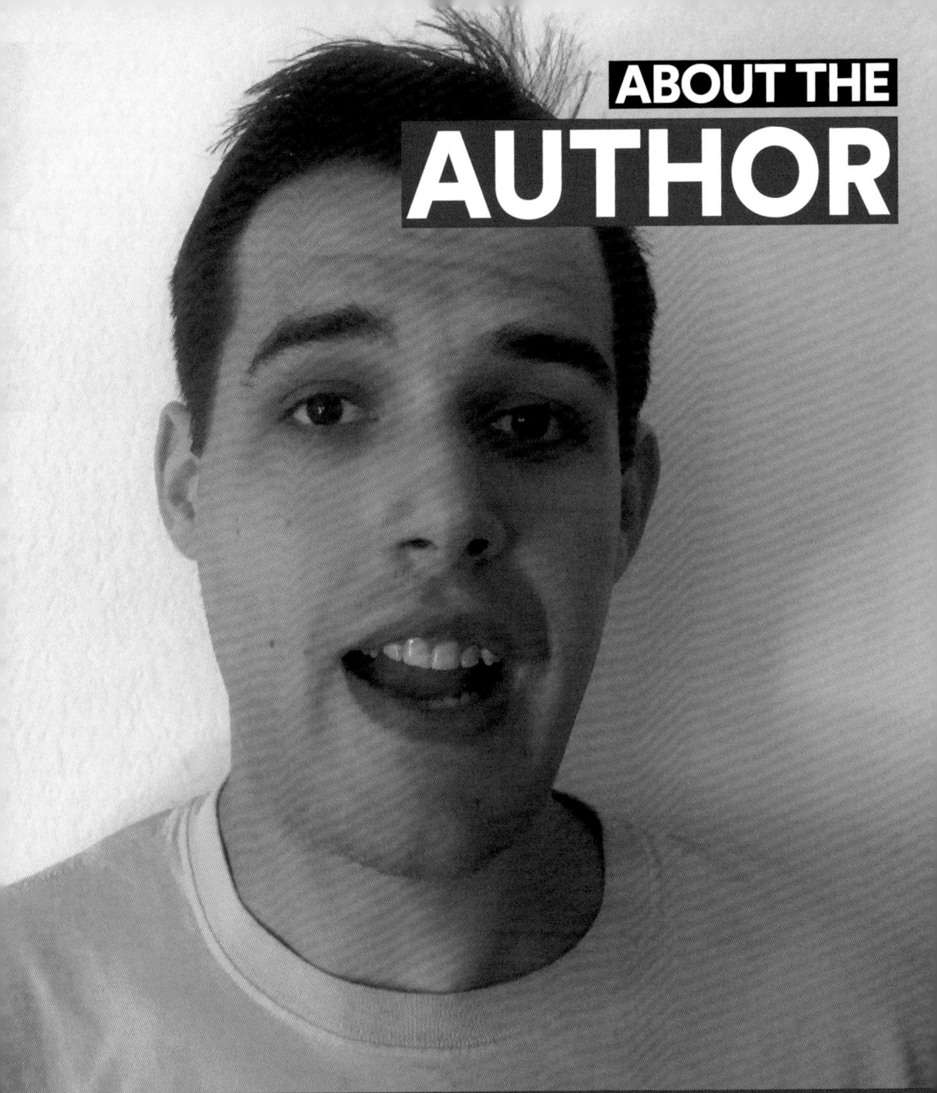

CARLTON HUDGENS currently resides in Las Vegas. He is employed part-time at Opportunity Village where he is responsible for putting together items for hotels on the Las Vegas Strip. Carlton assembles coffee creamers in packets, cuts out microfiche squares, and fills shampoos and conditioners in boxes.

BRIDGET HUDGENS is attending the University of Nevada, Las Vegas, where she is pursuing a bachelor of science degree in special education.

CARLTON...

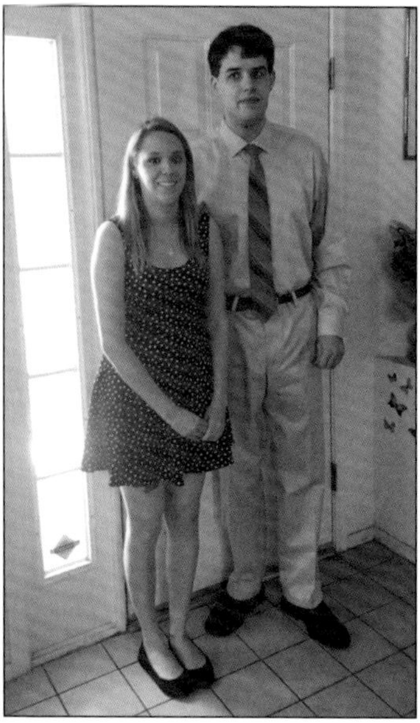

Carlton and I going to his favorite dance.

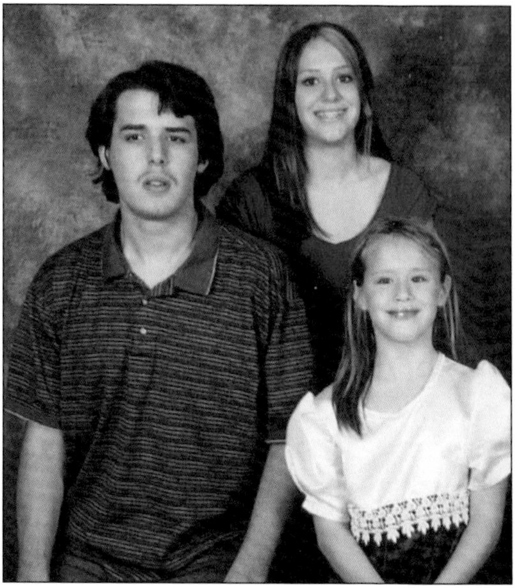

Family picture of Carlton, Candy, and me.

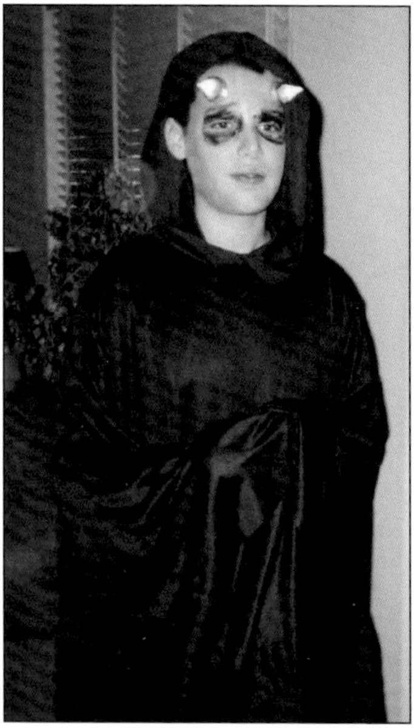

Carlton ready for Halloween.

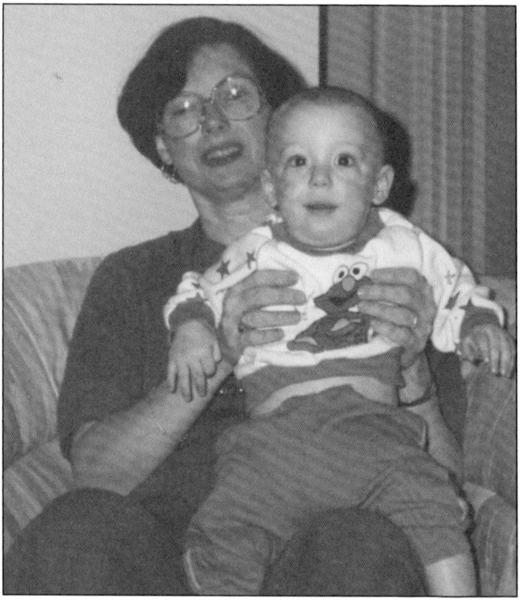

My lovely grandma Sally and my brother Carlton.

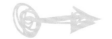

...CARLTON

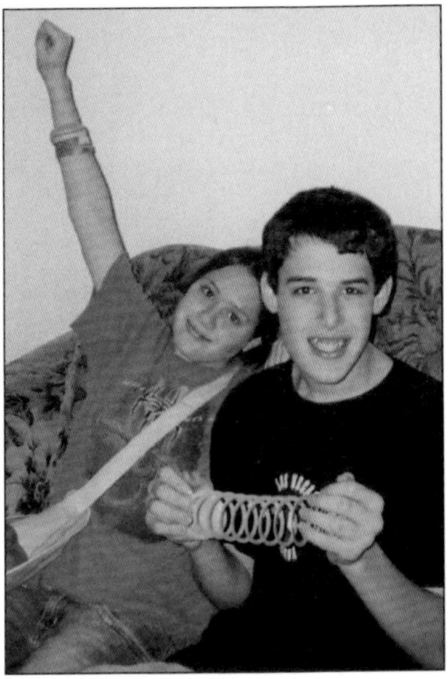

Carlton is all smiles on Christmas afternoon, enjoying his new presents.

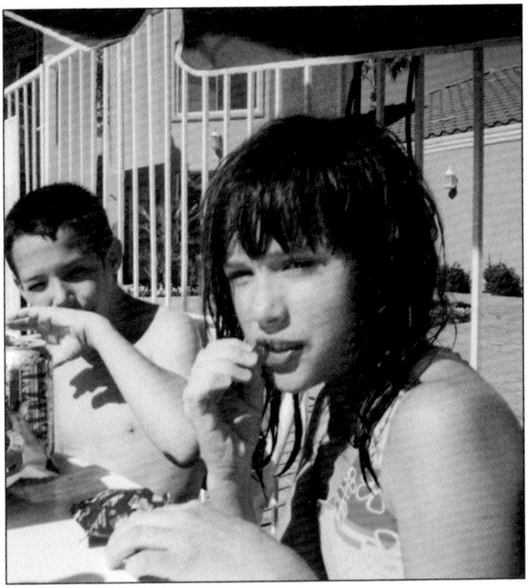

Carlton and I enjoy our favorite snacks at our favorite place—the pool!

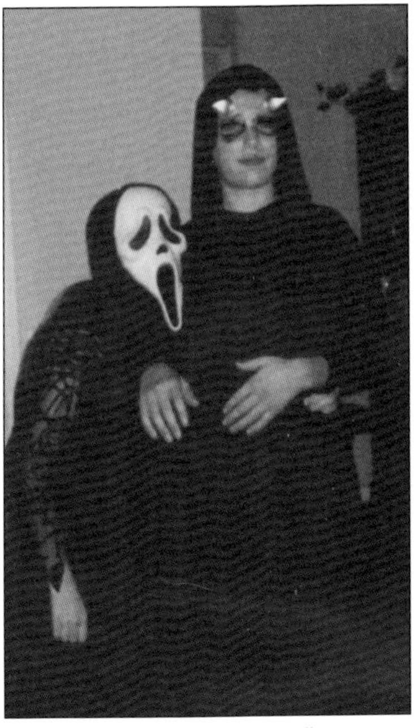

Carlton and I on our first Halloween at Nana and Papa's house.

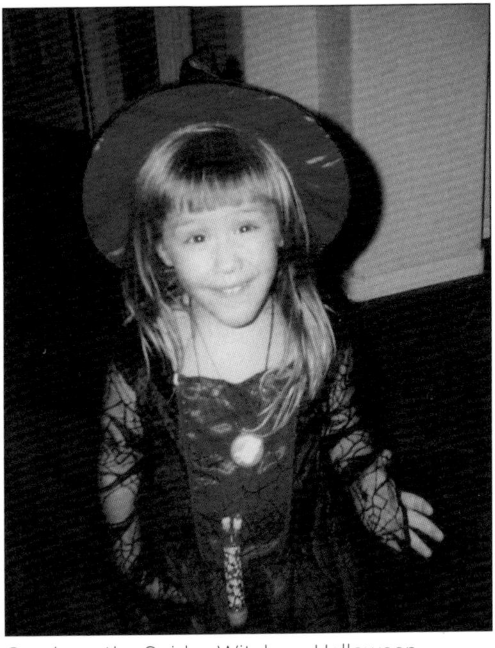

Candy as the Spider-Witch on Halloween.

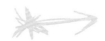

CARLTON...

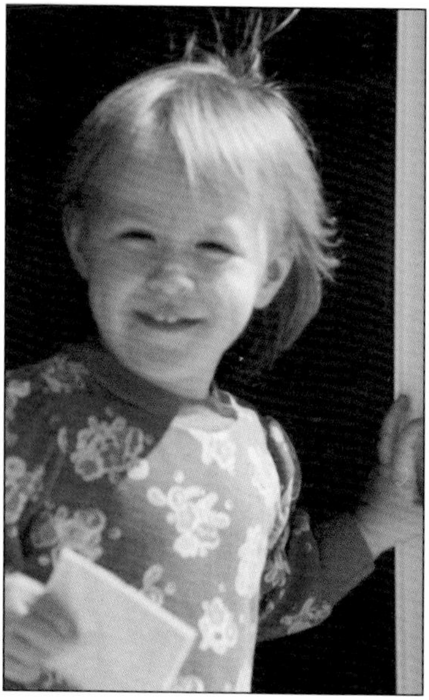

Candy getting ready to play outside.

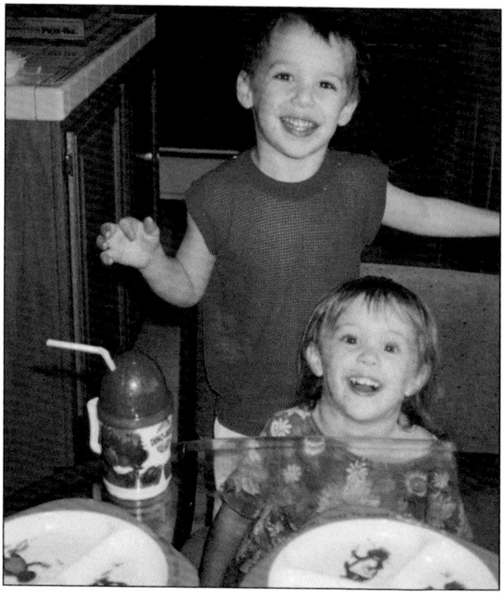

As kids, Carlton and I did everything together.

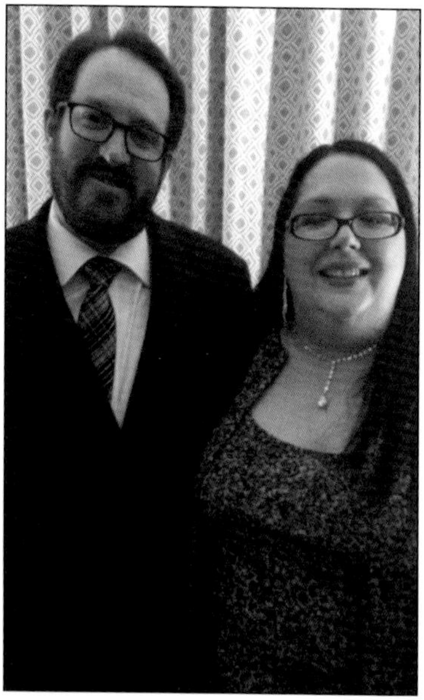

Mom and my new dad.

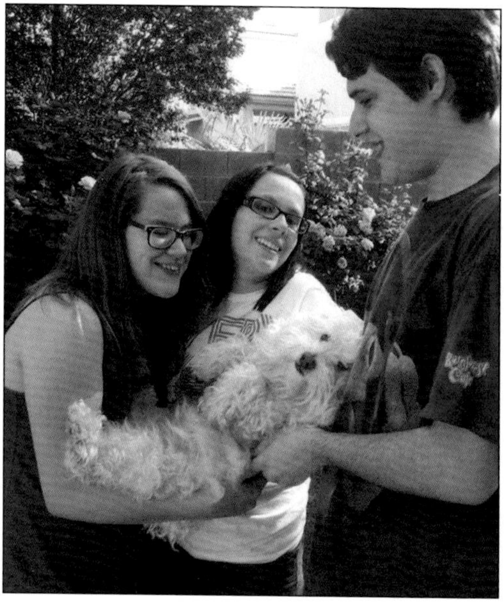

Carlton, Candy, and I with our family dog Mickie.

TAKE 5!

FIVE PARENT TAKE-AWAYS ABOUT AUTISM

CAROLYN BATTIN

is a former special education teacher at Vanderburg Elementary School in Henderson, Nevada, has worked with children with learning disabilities, including autism and those on the Asperger's spectrum, for thirty years.

AUTISM IS FASCINATING, AND CHALLENGING... IT IS NOT A CURSE.

When a child is first diagnosed with autism or Asperger's Syndrome, parents, teachers, and family members sometimes tend to stigmatize the child for having a disorder. But in fact, autism can be a gift. Many children with autism thrive in school, excel socially, and go on to be very successful in life.

FIND YOUR CHILD'S INNER BRILLIANCE.

Every child has something at which they excel. It may be reading, history, geography, art, math, video games, sports, board games . . . anything! Champion their cause (within reason) and try not to be judgmental. In many cases, that subject or activity may be the only thing that brings them any level of satisfaction or pride. Embrace it!

EVALUATION LEADS TO LIBERATION.

Many parents are in denial about their child having autism or being on the Asperger's spectrum, and are reluctant to have them evaluated, but it's better to know where your child is, than not understand why he is acting a certain way. Your child needs you to provide a base of understanding to help process a world that spins a hundred times faster than everyone else's.

BE YOUR CHILD'S BIGGEST ADVOCATE AND LOUDEST VOICE.

Just because your child has autism doesn't always mean she belongs in special ed, requires an aide, or needs a behavioral plan. Do not agree to any of these if the child's behavior is not impeding her ability to perform or learn in school. The range of assistance for a child is really on a case-by-case basis. Talk to your school district administrators about services available and use them only to your child's advantage.

STRIVE TOWARDS INDEPENDENCE.

Treat your children with autism like you treat your other children. Don't enable them or feel you need to protect them. Help them to be as independent as possible. Everyone needs to understand failure. Not every lesson needs to be a teaching opportunity. Give them the space to learn at their own level and their own pace. Remember, children on the spectrum just want to be loved and respected like any other child.

THE STORY
DOESN'T
END HERE...

VISIT
ZUIKERPRESS.COM

... to learn more about Bridget and Carlton's story, see behind-the-scenes videos of Bridget and Carlton and their family,

Our **WEBSITE** is another resource to help our readers deal with the issues that they face every day. Log on to find advice from experts, links to helpful organizations and literature, and more real-life experiences from young people just like you.

Spotlighting young writers with heartfelt stories that enlighten and inspire.

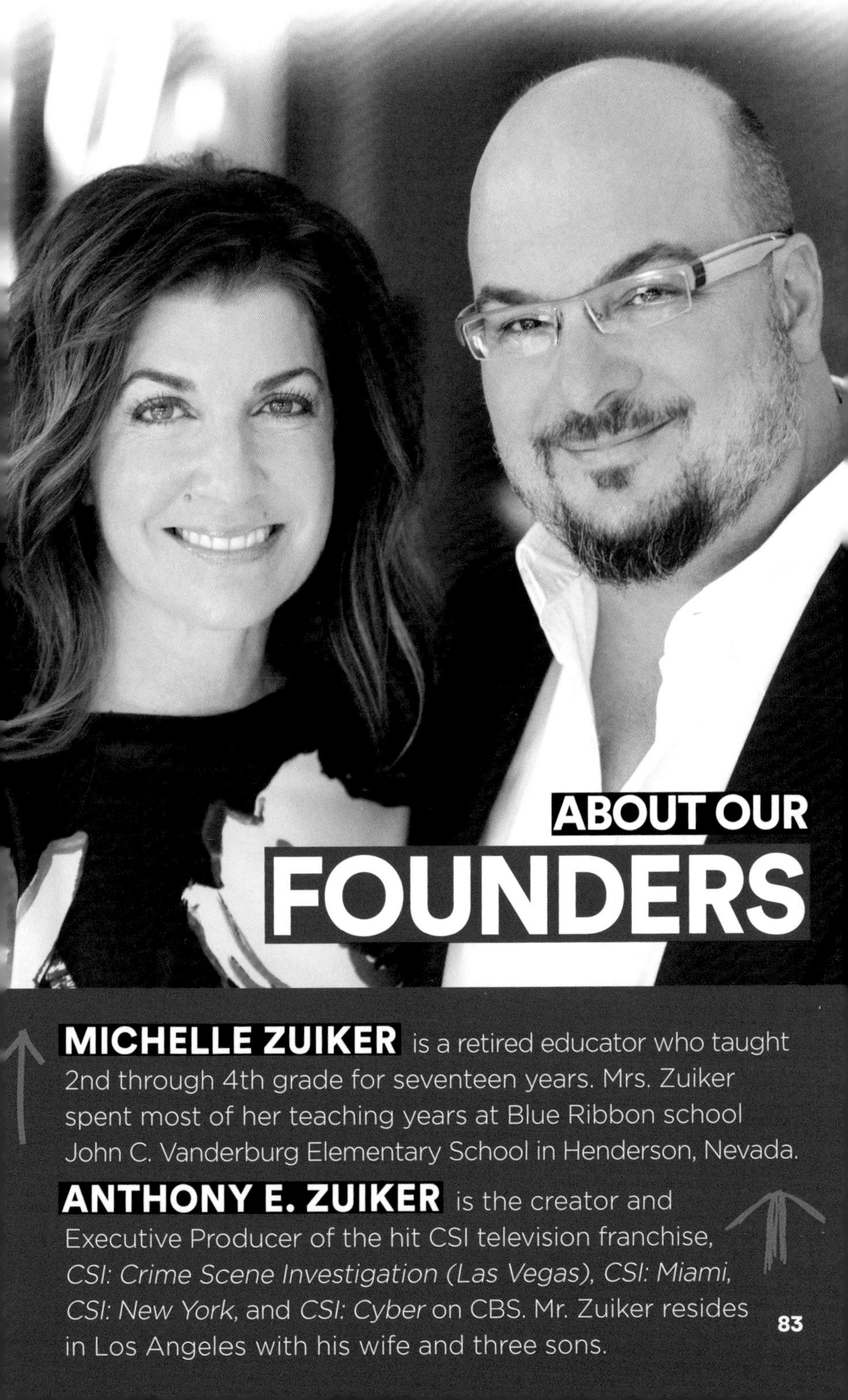

ABOUT OUR FOUNDERS

MICHELLE ZUIKER is a retired educator who taught 2nd through 4th grade for seventeen years. Mrs. Zuiker spent most of her teaching years at Blue Ribbon school John C. Vanderburg Elementary School in Henderson, Nevada.

ANTHONY E. ZUIKER is the creator and Executive Producer of the hit CSI television franchise, *CSI: Crime Scene Investigation (Las Vegas)*, *CSI: Miami*, *CSI: New York*, and *CSI: Cyber* on CBS. Mr. Zuiker resides in Los Angeles with his wife and three sons.

ABOUT OUR
ILLUSTRATORS
& EDITOR...

NAM KIM–PENCILER

is a Philadelphia-based artist, founder and director of Studio Imaginary Lines, an all-purpose design house which produces original content for comic books, video games, mobile apps and commercial advertising. Nam is a self-taught illustrator who credits artists such as Burne Hogarth, Jim Lee and Masamune Shiro for shaping his artistic style and vision. He has worked for Nike, ToykoPop, Radical Publishing and Image Comics where he illustrated the critically acclaimed *Samurai's Blood*.

FAHRIZA KAMAPUTRA–COLORIST

was born and raised in southern Jakarta. In 2010 he worked as colorist on a local comic book *Vienetta and the Stupid Aliens* which led to his work on the web comic *Rokki* and Madeleine Holly-Rosling's *Boston Metaphysical Society* with the studio STELLAR LABS. Fahriza now works as a freelance artist.

GARRY LEACH–COVER ARTIST

is a British artist best known for his work co-creating the new *Marvelman* with writer Alan Moore. As an artist Garry was a frequent contributor to *2000AD* working on *Dan Dare*, *Judge Dredd*, *The V.C.s* and *Future Shocks*. At DC Comics Garry worked on *Legion of Superheroes*, *Hit Man*, *Monarchy* and *Global Frequency*, while over at Marvel Comics, he inked Chris Weston on *The Twelve*. Garry has been a cover artist for Marvel, DC, *2000AD*, *Eclipse*, *Dynamic Forces*, and Kellogg's Corn Flakes.

DAVE ELLIOTT–EDITOR

has more than thirty-five years of experience working and garnering awards in every aspect of the entertainment industry, from writer and artist, to editor and publisher. Dave has worked on diverse titles such as *A1*, *Deadline*, *Viz Comic*, *Heavy Metal* magazine, *2000AD*, *Justice League of America*, *Transformers*, *GI Joe*, the *Real Ghostbusters* and *Doctor Who*. He also developed projects for Johnny Depp, Dwayne Johnson, and Tom Cruise. Through his own company, AtomekArt, Dave has created his own graphic novel series, *Odyssey* and *The Weirding Willows*.

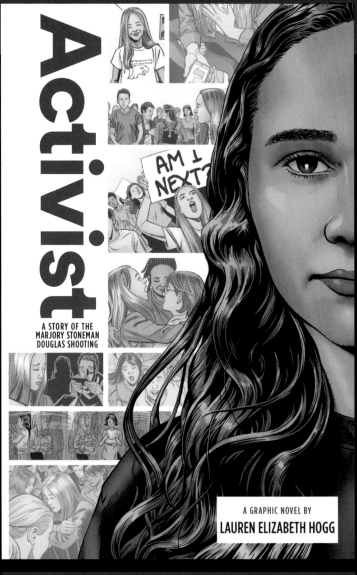

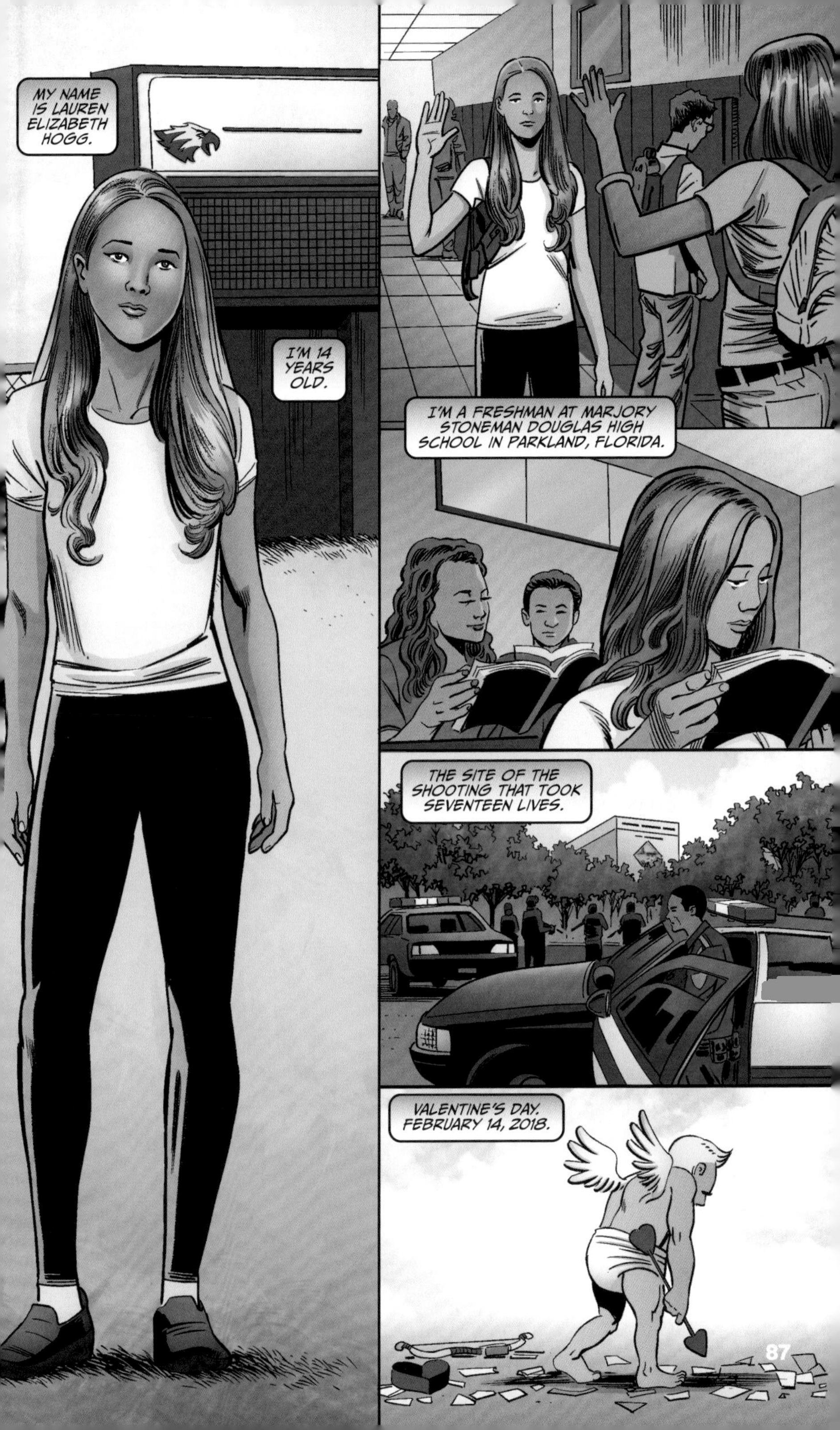
MY NAME IS LAUREN ELIZABETH HOGG.
I'M 14 YEARS OLD.
I'M A FRESHMAN AT MARJORY STONEMAN DOUGLAS HIGH SCHOOL IN PARKLAND, FLORIDA.
THE SITE OF THE SHOOTING THAT TOOK SEVENTEEN LIVES.
VALENTINE'S DAY. FEBRUARY 14, 2018.

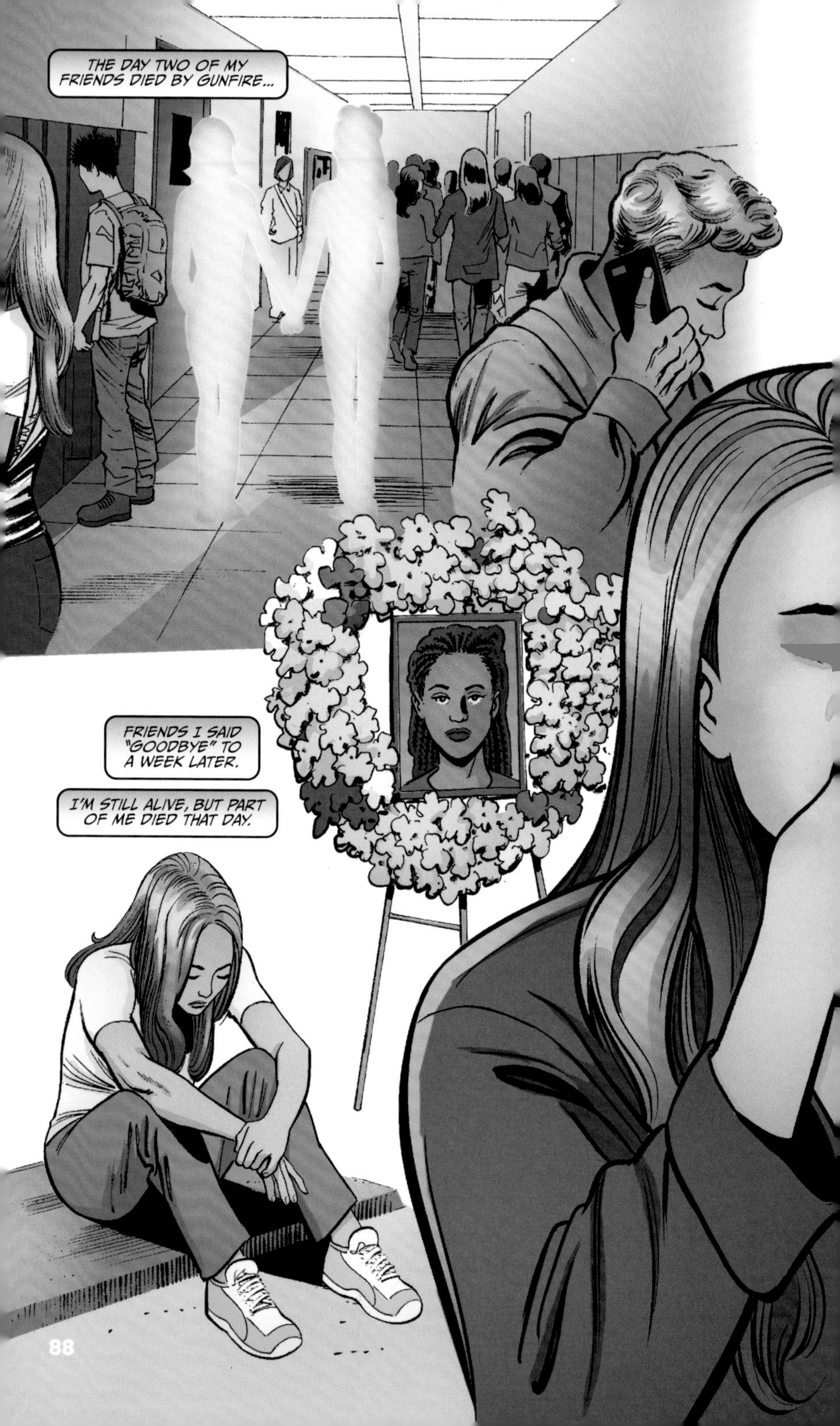
THE DAY TWO OF MY FRIENDS DIED BY GUNFIRE...
FRIENDS I SAID "GOODBYE" TO A WEEK LATER.
I'M STILL ALIVE, BUT PART OF ME DIED THAT DAY.

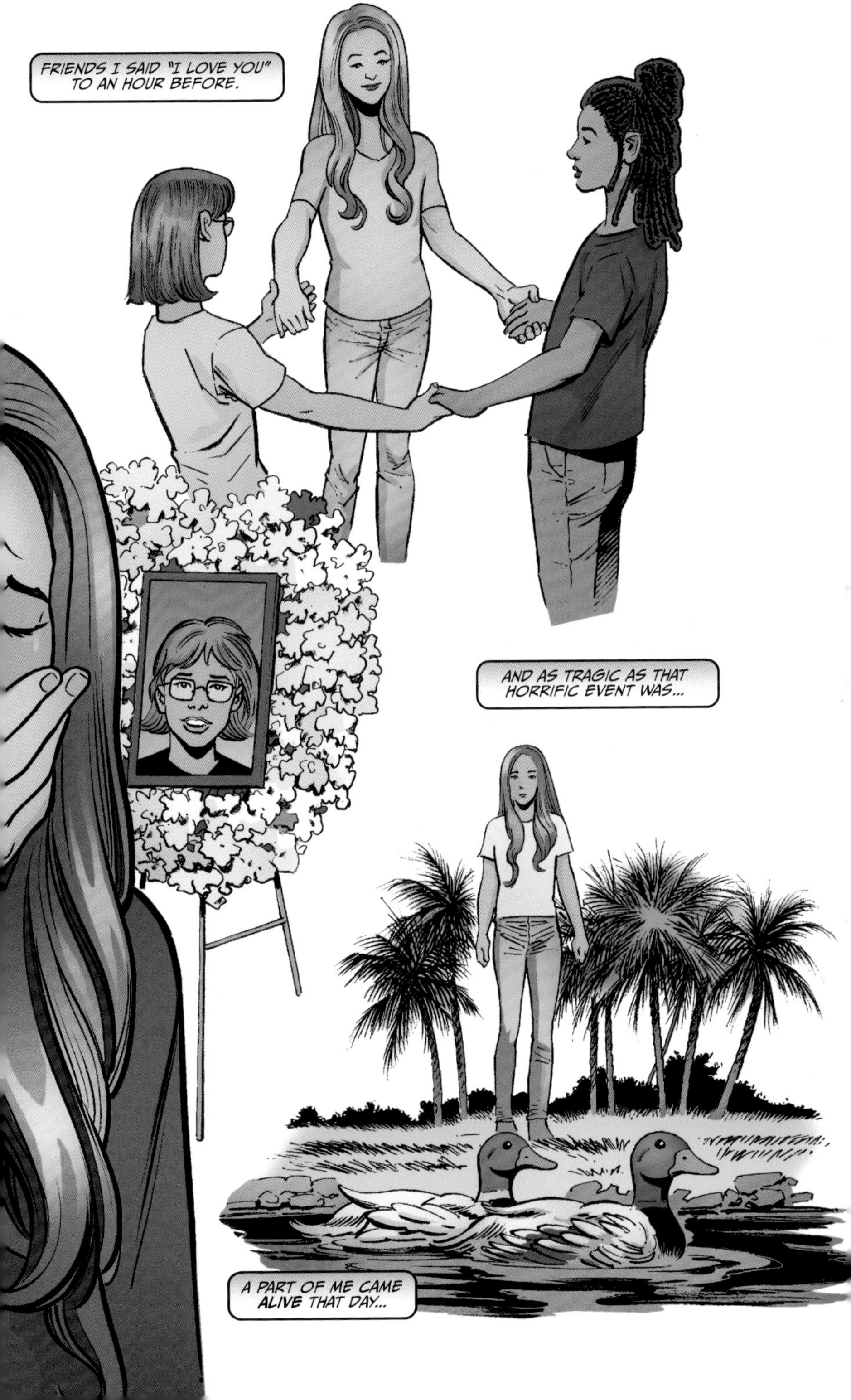
FRIENDS I SAID "I LOVE YOU" TO AN HOUR BEFORE.
AND AS TRAGIC AS THAT HORRIFIC EVENT WAS...
A PART OF ME CAME ALIVE THAT DAY...

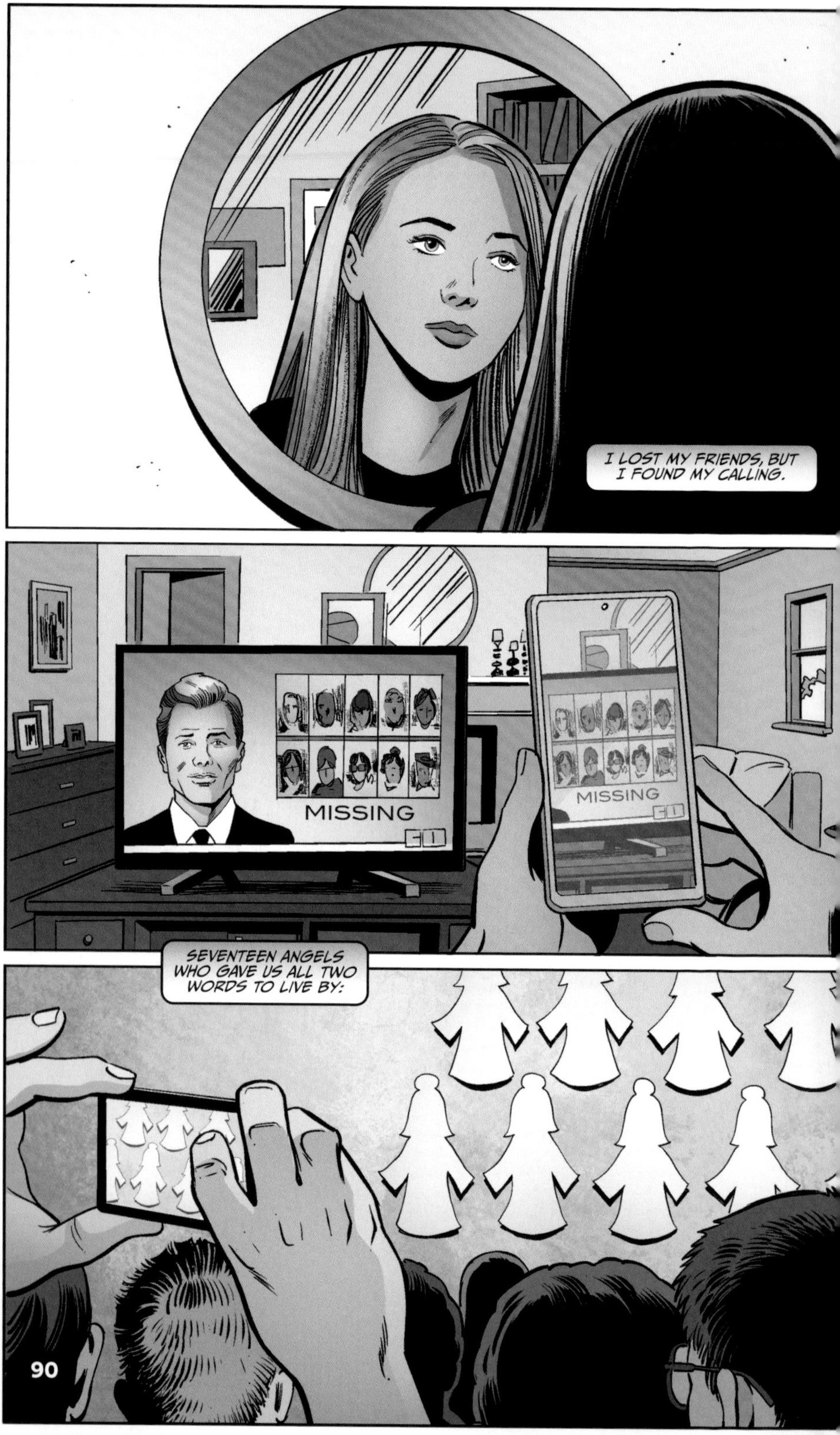
I LOST MY FRIENDS, BUT I FOUND MY CALLING.
MISSING
MISSING
SEVENTEEN ANGELS WHO GAVE US ALL TWO WORDS TO LIVE BY:

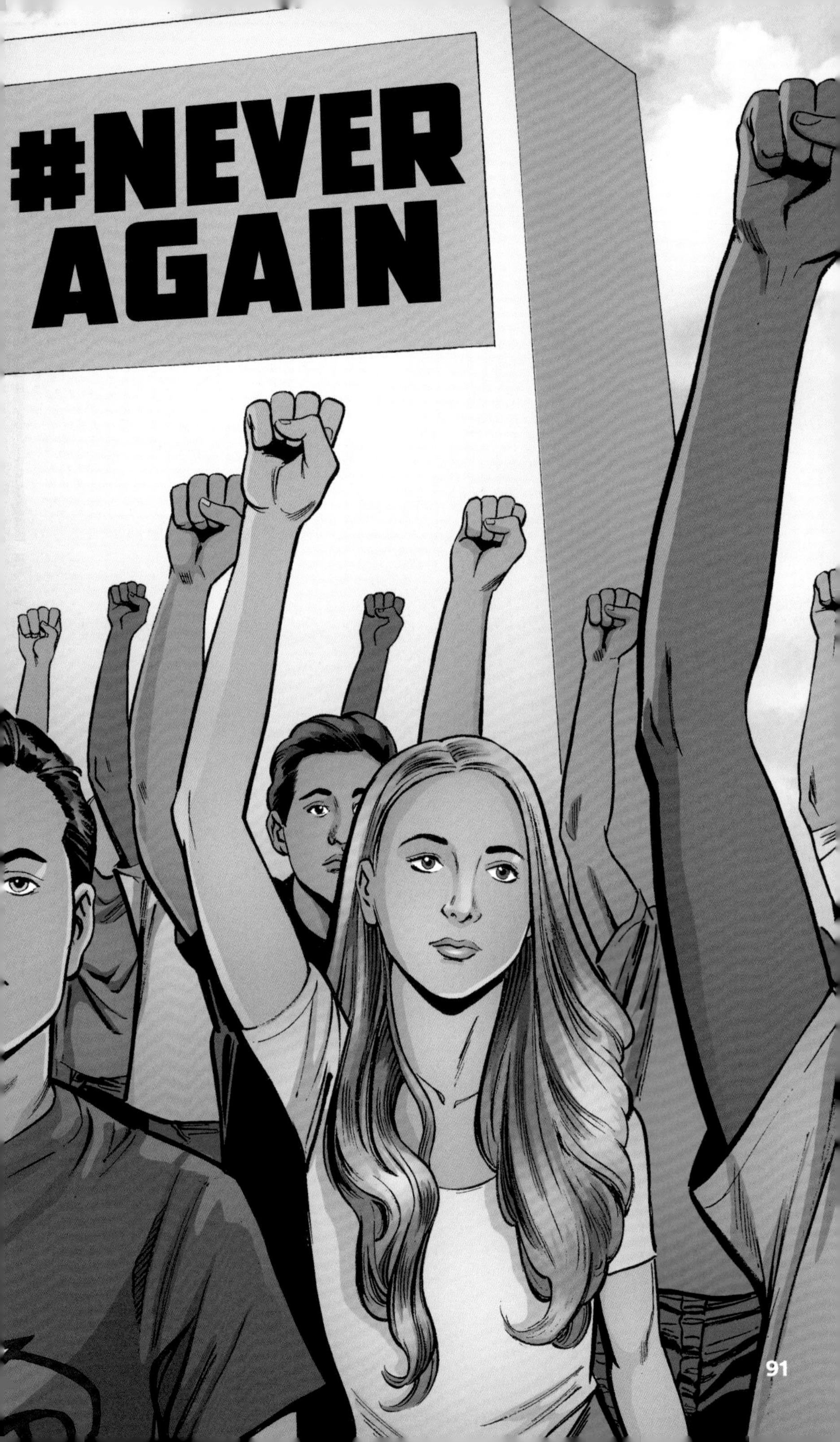
#NEVER AGAIN

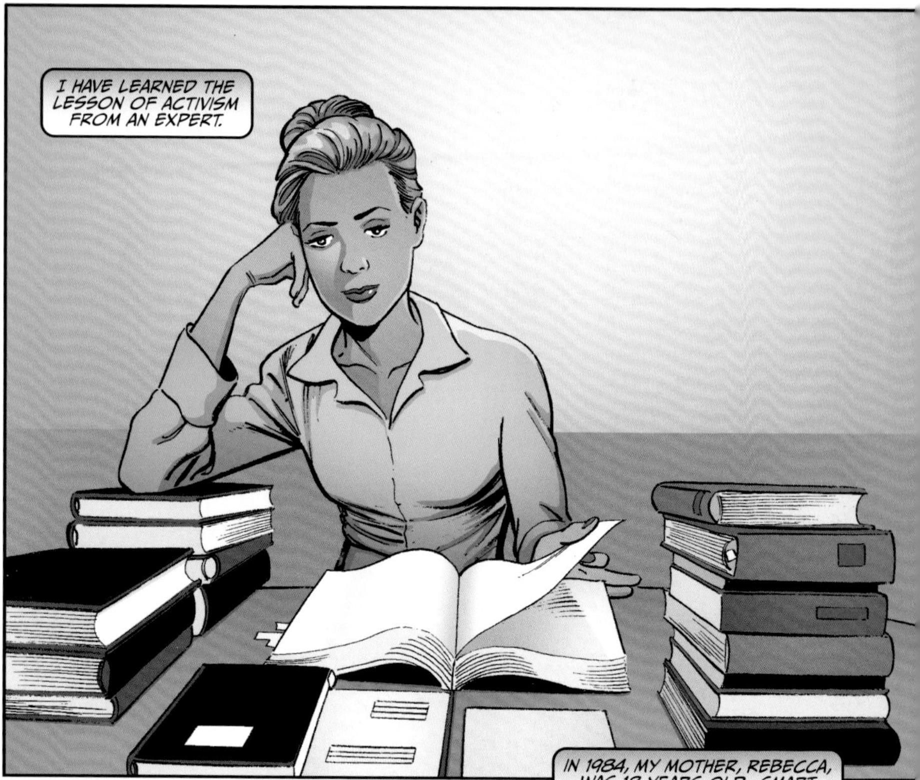
I HAVE LEARNED THE LESSON OF ACTIVISM FROM AN EXPERT.

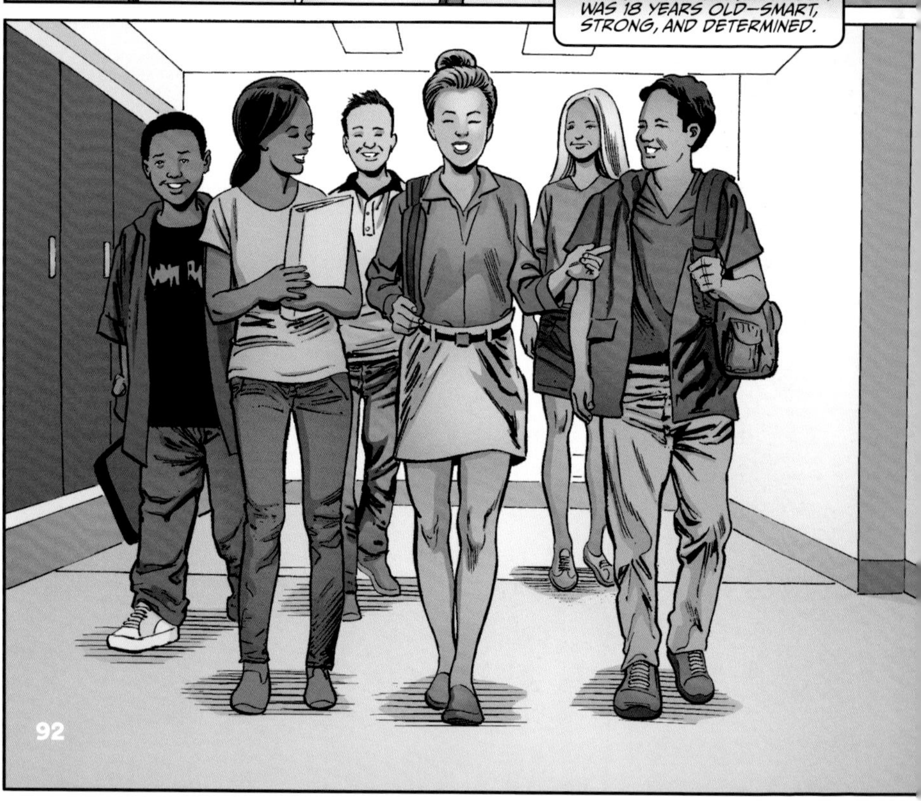
IN 1984, MY MOTHER, REBECCA, WAS 18 YEARS OLD—SMART, STRONG, AND DETERMINED.

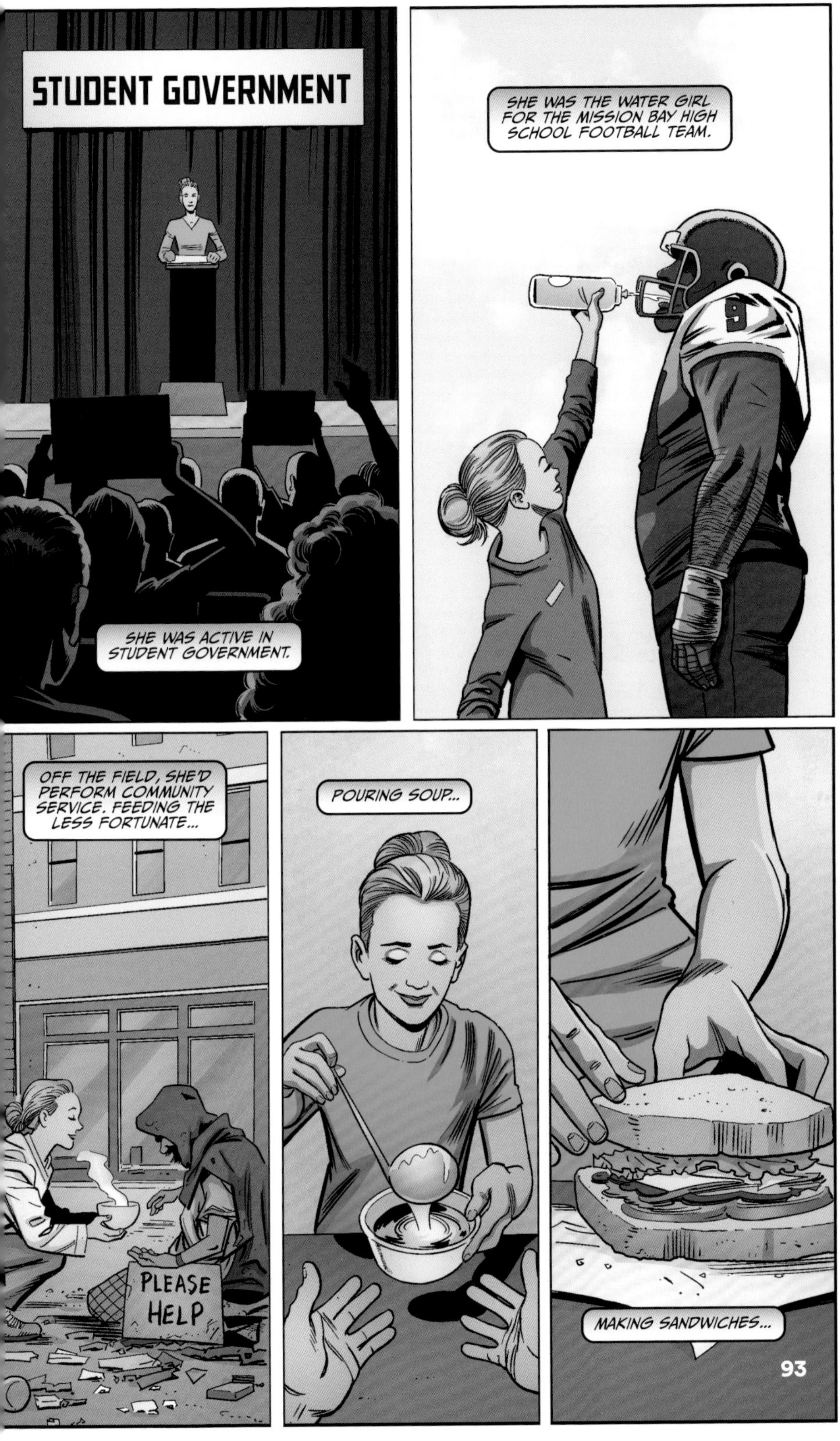
STUDENT GOVERNMENT
SHE WAS ACTIVE IN STUDENT GOVERNMENT.
SHE WAS THE WATER GIRL FOR THE MISSION BAY HIGH SCHOOL FOOTBALL TEAM.
OFF THE FIELD, SHE'D PERFORM COMMUNITY SERVICE. FEEDING THE LESS FORTUNATE...
PLEASE HELP
POURING SOUP...
MAKING SANDWICHES...

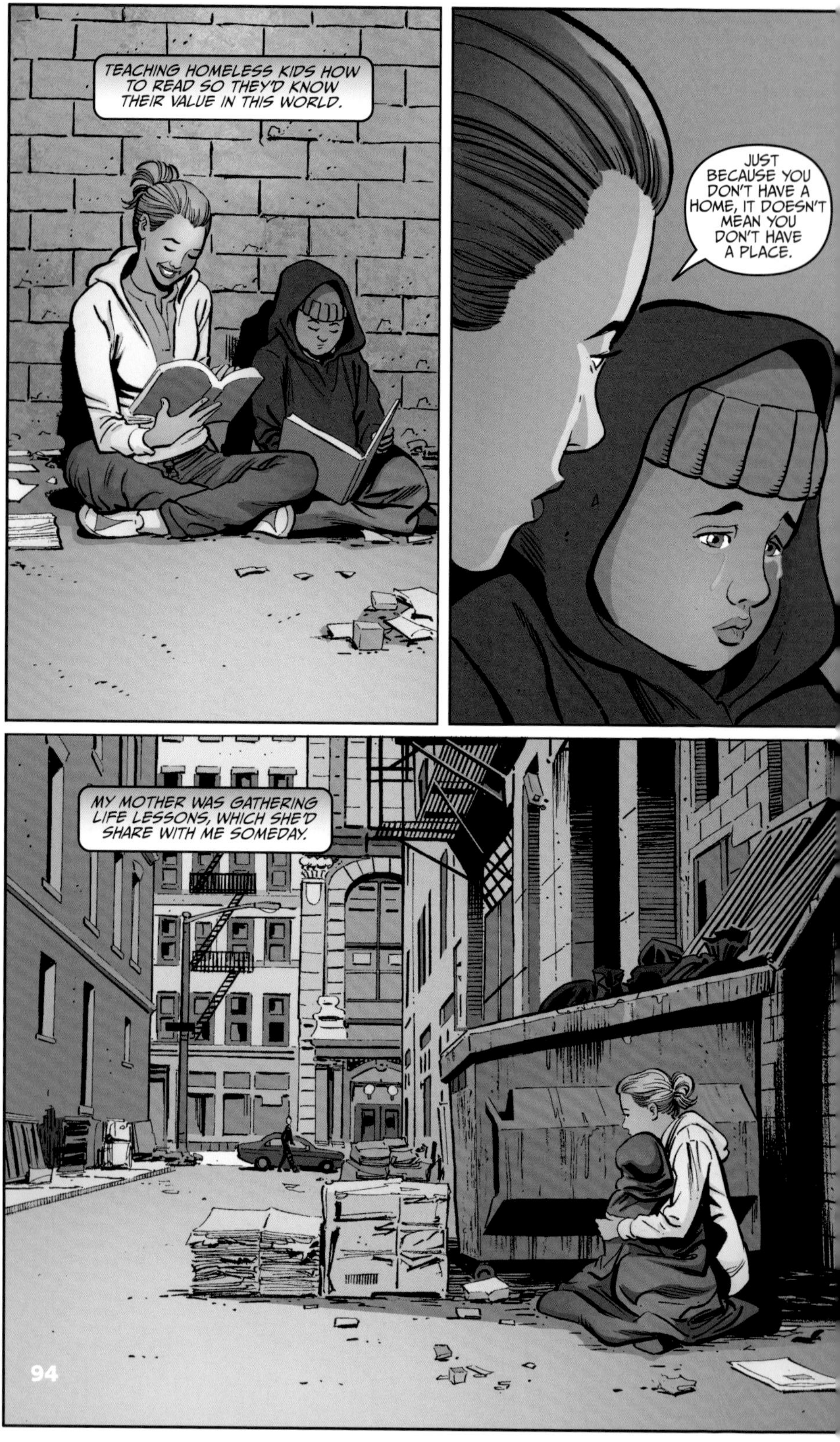
TEACHING HOMELESS KIDS HOW TO READ SO THEY'D KNOW THEIR VALUE IN THIS WORLD.
JUST BECAUSE YOU DON'T HAVE A HOME, IT DOESN'T MEAN YOU DON'T HAVE A PLACE.
MY MOTHER WAS GATHERING LIFE LESSONS, WHICH SHE'D SHARE WITH ME SOMEDAY.

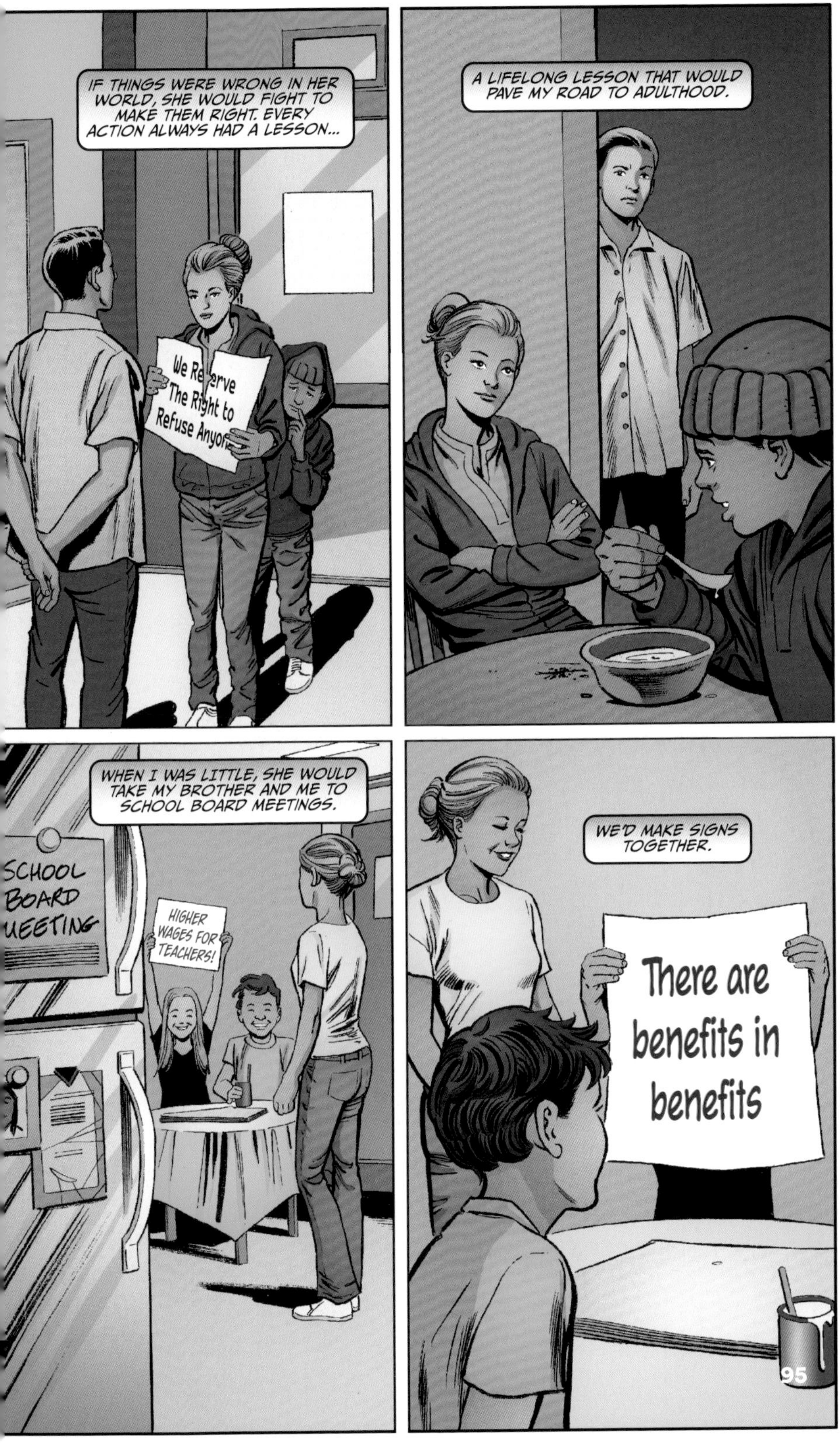

IF THINGS WERE WRONG IN HER WORLD, SHE WOULD FIGHT TO MAKE THEM RIGHT. EVERY ACTION ALWAYS HAD A LESSON...
We Re erve The Right to Refuse Anyon
A LIFELONG LESSON THAT WOULD PAVE MY ROAD TO ADULTHOOD.
WHEN I WAS LITTLE, SHE WOULD TAKE MY BROTHER AND ME TO SCHOOL BOARD MEETINGS.
SCHOOL BOARD MEETING
HIGHER WAGES FOR TEACHERS!
WE'D MAKE SIGNS TOGETHER.
There are benefits in benefits

NEW FOR FALL 2019

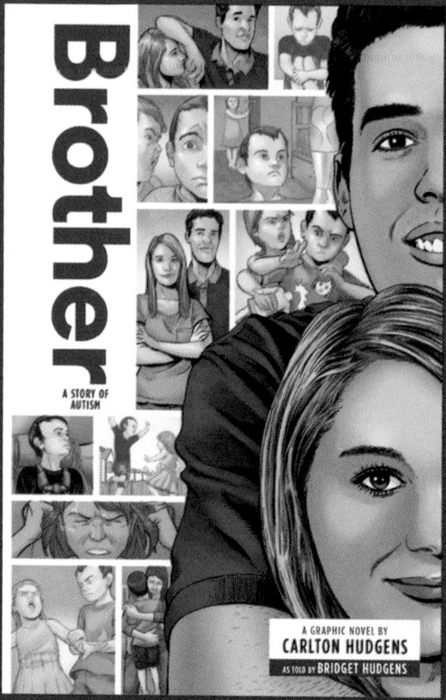
Brother
A STORY OF AUTISM
A GRAPHIC NOVEL BY
CARLTON HUDGENS
AS TOLD BY BRIDGET HUDGENS

BROTHER: A STORY OF AUTISM

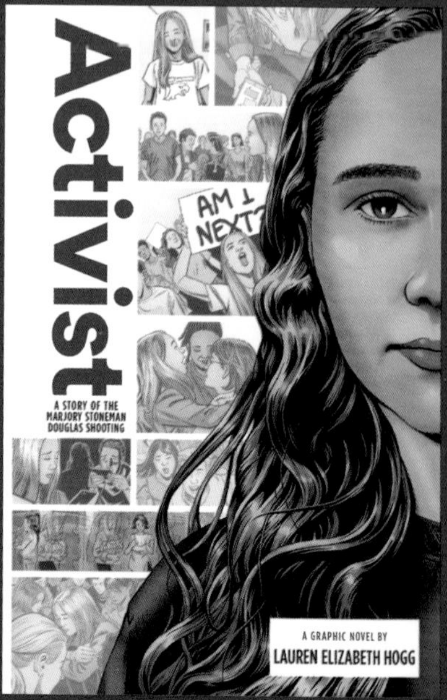
Activist
AM I NEXT?
A STORY OF THE MARJORY STONEMAN DOUGLAS SHOOTING
A GRAPHIC NOVEL BY
LAUREN ELIZABETH HOGG

ACTIVIST: A STORY OF THE MARJORY STONEMAN DOUGLAS SHOOTING

COMING SPRING 2020

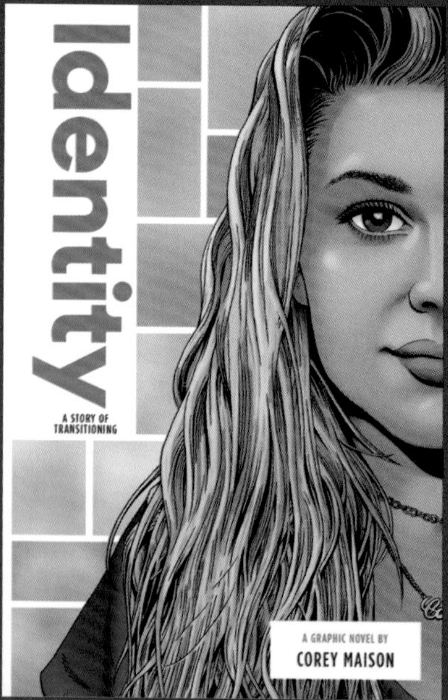
Identity
A STORY OF TRANSITIONING
A GRAPHIC NOVEL BY
COREY MAISON

IDENTITY: A STORY OF TRANSITIONING

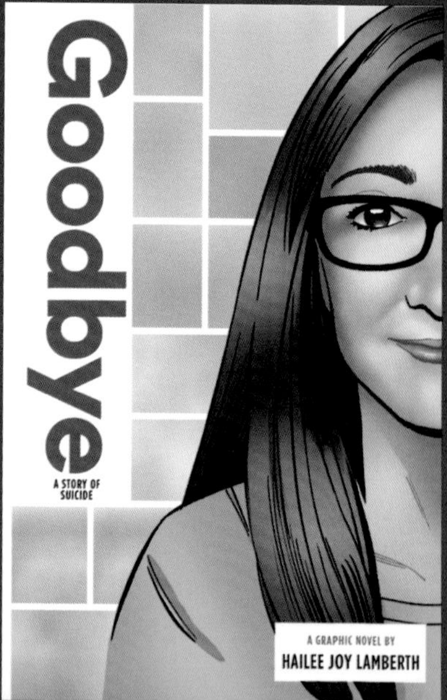
Goodbye
A STORY OF SUICIDE
A GRAPHIC NOVEL BY
HAILEE JOY LAMBERTH

GOODBYE: A STORY OF SUICIDE